# INTENTIONAL CHILDREN

RAISING MONEY-SMART, MINDFUL KIDS OF
INTENTION AND PURPOSE

KALEN BRUCE

Copyright © 2020 by Kalen Bruce.

All rights reserved. No part of this work may be reproduced, distributed, or transmitted in any form or by any means, without prior written permission.

For permission to use any part of this work, please contact the author at freedomsprout.com.

ISBN: 978-1-7349734-3-3

Library of Congress Control Number: 2020911606

All content reflects the author's opinion at a given time and can change as time progresses. All information should be taken as an opinion and should not be misconstrued for professional or legal advice. The contents of this book are informational in nature and are not legal or tax advice, and the author is not engaged in the provision of legal, tax, or any other advice.

The views presented in this book are those of the author and do not necessarily represent the views of DoD or its components.

The stories in this book are real-life, true stories, but many of the names and roles have been changed for the sake of anonymity.

Scripture quotations are from the ESV® Bible (The Holy Bible, English Standard Version®), copyright © 2001 by Crossway Bibles, a publishing ministry of Good News Publishers. Used by permission. All rights reserved.

Printed by Kalen Bruce in the United States of America.

First printing edition 2020. Hot Springs, Arkansas.

# PRAISE FOR INTENTIONAL CHILDREN

"If you are a parent and want your kids to get a grip on money earlier than you did (don't we all?) then you will love *Intentional Children*. Kalen has a heart of a loving teacher and is a goldmine of wisdom when it comes to helping parents raise money-smart kids."

BOB LOTICH, CEPF®, FOUNDER OF SEEDTIME AND<br>BEST-SELLING AUTHOR

"Kalen Bruce knows about money and kids-- he and his spouse are raising five of them. His book helps you show your kids how to manage their money. Better yet, you'll learn how to build their mindset around the important parts of life! They'll avoid the toy traps and tech hazards to focus on family, gratitude, and living with purpose. Along the way, his techniques will improve your mindset and finances too."

DOUG NORDMAN, AUTHOR OF *THE MILITARY GUIDE* AND CO-AUTHOR OF *RAISING YOUR MONEY-SAVVY FAMILY*

"As a parent of a young adult who has walked with my husband and me through debt recovery, I can validate the wisdom in these words from Kalen's book, 'Any time the opportunity presents itself to show your child how you did something smart with money, or made a financial mistake, use it to teach. Your kids will see what you do before they'll hear what you say. Since we can't turn back time, we can do the next best thing: teach our children the things we wish we had learned at a young age. ' *Intentional Children* was written to instruct parents on how to train their children about money, but any reader of any age or season of life can greatly benefit from its wisdom. Though Kalen lays out very specific steps to follow to successfully prepare children for the real world and how to handle finances, his advice applies to so many other areas of life. I love that he writes from a Christian, Biblical perspective and that he gently incorporates his faith throughout the book. Kalen says, 'I've done the majority of the leg work for you,' and the sharing of what he has gleaned from doing that leg work is an invaluable gift for those who will read this book."

CHERYL E. SMITH, AUTHOR OF *BIBLICAL MINIMALISM*

"*Intentional Children* by Kalen Bruce is one of the most refreshing books I have read in awhile. It approaches difficult topics like financial literacy and parenting in a way that is not only relatable, but also actionable. A very easy read and much needed especially in a time where there is so much uncertainty, being intentional is more important than ever!"

LORNE JENKINS, CEO OF MINI MONEY MANAGEMENT

## CONTENTS

Acknowledgments — ix
Author's Note — xiii
Introduction — xv

**PART ONE**
**MONEY**

1. Reframing Money — 3
2. Teaching Money — 19
3. Money Lessons — 33
4. Work Ethic — 63
5. Money Management — 75
6. Transportation — 83
7. The Debt Trap — 103
8. College Conversations — 115
9. Investing — 137

**PART TWO**
**MINDSET**

10. Intentional Ownership — 151
11. The Toy Trap — 163
12. Ad Alert — 171
13. The Technology Threat — 183
14. Growing Gratitude — 199
15. Rethinking Presents — 213
16. God-Centered Home — 227
17. Intentional Days — 235

Afterword — 249
About Kalen Bruce — 257
Also by Kalen Bruce — 259
Notes — 261

## ACKNOWLEDGMENTS

Thank you to everyone who has formed me and shaped me into the man God called me to be. There are too many to name. Most importantly, thank you to my wife, Tiffany, for putting up with my insanely early writing hours every morning. Thanks for dealing with me when it feels like you have six children.

A special thank you to my mother, Cindy, for always loving, caring for, and serving me. You have a servant's heart. It's who you are and it's beautiful.

Thank you to my other parents, Brenda and James, for always believing in me and supporting our family. You have both inspired me in more ways than you will ever know.

Thanks to all of the editors and early readers who had a hand in making this book better. Thanks to MK Williams for coaching me through the entire process of publishing this book, and it was a process.

Finally, I acknowledge I am only capable of learning, thinking, and writing because of God. I give the highest praise to Jesus Christ for continuing to mold me to his vision for my life. That's the vision I want to live out and the vision I want to pass down to my kids.

*To my children: Abi, Asher, Hannah, Jezreel, and Josiah. You are the reason these thoughts become pages in a book. You are my motivation for raising a generation of money-smart, intentional kids, and my motivation for intentional living in my own life. My goal to reach 1,000,000 children starts with you five.*

# AUTHOR'S NOTE

My beliefs do not dictate how you receive the message in this book. I am a Christian, and this book is written from a biblical perspective, but this is not a *Christian* book. You don't have to be a Christian to practice and use the principles I teach. They apply to families across the globe, and they transcend all worldviews. As a financial coach, I've worked with people of all different beliefs and backgrounds, and my own beliefs have never caused tension. I back up the things I write with research. Chapter 16 is the only chapter directed specifically at Christians, but I still believe you can get value from that chapter regardless of your beliefs. We don't have to agree on everything. We should learn and grow together—with each other, from each other.

# INTRODUCTION

This book is about intentional living: an uncommon way of life. Most people go through life doing whatever they think they should, based on what everyone else is doing. This book is about being different. Living differently. Living intentionally.

In Part 1, you'll learn how and what to teach your kids about money. If you feel like you don't know much about money, don't worry. You may be surprised by how simple some of this stuff is, and how easy it is to teach it to your kids. Part 2 is all about instilling a healthy mindset in our kids for how to view money and the rest of the world. We'll go over all kinds of topics many people never stop to think about. This isn't a basic parenting book. I'm not going to talk about discipline and many other aspects of parenting. There are plenty of great books on parenting. I wrote this book to hit all of the in-between points that other books have missed, like teaching kids about money, buying their first car, how advertising affects your kids, how having fewer toys leads to happier kids, and family time management. Topics that don't seem to be part of common parenting books.

With any topic in this book (and most topics in life), there are caveats. Much of my writing is straightforward and to the point. My goal is to give you the information in a concise, conversational, and simple way. If I spent the time to consider caveats in every situation, this book would be 800 pages long. Nobody wants that. So just know, every situation in this book will not be handled and viewed the same way by everybody. I don't expect you to agree with me on every point. That's ok. We're all uniquely created. This is especially true of Part 1. It's called *personal* finance, because it's exactly that: personal.

Finally, I want to mention "the curse of knowledge," an idea popularized by Chip and Dan Heath. The curse of knowledge is the idea that when a person knows something, it's difficult for him or her to explain it, because the teacher's level of understanding is much deeper than the learner's, and the teacher often doesn't even realize it. The *knowledge* of a subject *curses* our ability to explain it in terms people can understand. Think of trying to explain your specialty to someone who knows nothing about it. You've done the research and poured hours into a subject. Trying to explain all of that to someone in one conversation (or one book) is tough, to say the least. We tend to use complicated jargon without even realizing it. It's important to be aware of this when teaching anything.

In writing this book, I took the curse of knowledge into account and decided, based on feedback and research, to break things down into simple terms, *spaced out throughout the book.* Sometimes it might seem like I'm repeating myself—that means it's important. Many of the topics in Part 1 are complex, and I do my best to simplify them. However, if you're completely unfamiliar with a topic, it's not going to help you if I go on for pages and pages. That's why this book is set up to give you a bite of a topic, and then later, we'll come back and you'll learn a little more. This is to help you stay engaged and learn gradually. We tend to learn best when information is pieced together slowly—throughout an entire book, for example. We should teach our children the same way: slowly, over their entire lives.

Let's begin.

# PART ONE
# MONEY

## ONE
# REFRAMING MONEY
### FROM TABOO TO TEACHABLE MOMENTS

"In these story telling moments we equip our children with crucial solution tools for life. To deprive them of these necessary teachable moments is like denying a carpenter the tools of his trade."

DREXEL DEAL, FROM *THE FIGHT OF MY LIFE IS WRAPPED UP IN MY FATHER*

"It is easier to build strong children than to repair broken men."

FREDERICK DOUGLASS, SOCIAL REFORMER AND ABOLITIONIST

---

"I'M TRANSFERRING ALL MY MONEY OVER TO A CREDIT UNION," SAID a 19-year-old I recently met.

"Why's that?" I asked him.

"Because credit unions are supposed to be better than banks. You know, for interest rates and stuff," he replied.

A 21-year-old overheard the conversation. She decided to chime in and said, "I just got a credit card with 3% cashback on all my purchases. I don't worry about my savings account rate, because my cashback rate is higher than the savings accounts I've looked up. As long as I use this card I'm earning 3% on my money."

Conversations like this show why kids need financial education before they move out on their own. It's not that credit unions and credit cards are bad. The problem is, he knows just enough about credit unions to be talked into a loan he doesn't need, because he "heard credit unions are supposed to be better." And she knows just enough about credit cards to fall into debt, paying high interest rates on her balance, while chasing that 3% cashback.

When kids enter the real world with "just enough" information, they'll soon find they don't know enough to make informed financial decisions. Knowing a little bit about a handful of financial products is a disaster waiting to happen. Sometimes knowing a little makes us think we're informed enough to make a big decision.

Personal finance isn't a priority in the American education system. A colossal 99% of American adults agree finance should be taught in the classroom, so why does it seem like it's not taught in 99% of schools?

Financial journalist Dan Kadlec pointed out a few reasons why finance isn't taught in schools, in *Time* magazine.[1] There are five primary reasons:

1. **Qualification** – Only one in five teachers feels qualified to lead a personal finance class.
2. **Instructor Shortage** – We don't have enough instructors to teach the class in the first place.
3. **Standardized Tests** – Personal finance isn't part of the ACT or SAT – if it's not tested, it's not taught.
4. **State Guidelines** – Education is up to each individual state, and each state has different ideas on what should and shouldn't be part of the curriculum.
5. **General Disagreement** – Nobody seems to be able to agree on which principles should be taught if we did have the class.

It's hard to pinpoint the real reason it's not taught in schools, but the fact remains: *financial education for children is the responsibility of the parents.* We can't rely on the school system for it. This creates another problem, because if most teachers don't feel qualified to teach finance classes, how do parents feel?

Most parents could use substantial help in this department. Eighty percent of adults in the U.S. say they could use help with financial questions, according to a 2012 study,[2] and it seems to be getting worse. Just talk to your neighbor, a colleague, or the first person you see on the street, and see how they're doing with their money. The average person has less than $1,000 in savings, if that tells you anything.[3]

If we're responsible for teaching financial skills to our children, we need to get our finances together. It takes some self-education, but it pays off exponentially for generations to come.

When parents are bad with money, the cure-all advice to their kids is typically, "go to college and get good grades so you can get a good job," but this alone doesn't solve the problem.

According to doctor and writer Sanj Katyal, M.D., most doctors have no clue what they're doing with their money.[4] So much for being wealthy from your profession alone. Money doesn't simply solve money problems, because the problem is rarely the amount of money someone has; it's what they do with that money.

It's common for someone who isn't doing well financially (and didn't go to college) to think the answer for their children is a college education. It goes something like this: "Go to college like I never did so you'll be successful like I never was." It seems legitimate, and I'm sure the best intentions are there, but that doesn't mean it's the right answer. There is nothing wrong with college—we'll talk about getting a debt-free degree later—but we have to prepare our kids to handle their finances *before* they leave for college. Unless they're going to school for a finance degree, college won't teach your children about money either. They could end up with a high income and no clue how to handle it (observe the typical NFL or NBA player… or doctor). It all starts with small conversations. We have to talk about it, and therein lies a major issue: we don't.

## We Don't Talk About Money

Money is often a taboo subject. As children, we're taught to never discuss our personal finances, and to not ask questions about others' finances. Money is a private issue. You don't discuss your income, your investments, or your savings. You just don't do it. You *never* talk about your personal finances. That's why kids know absolutely nothing about their parents' financial situation, which leads to adults who know nothing about finances in general. That's where most people stop.

Honestly, that's where most people *are* right now. They're struggling to make it and are afraid to ask for help because they don't want anyone else to see their finances.

I grew up in the we-don't-talk-about-money generation. Actually, it seems like that's been every generation. My parents didn't talk about money, but their parents *really* didn't talk about money. Somewhere along the way it became the norm to keep kids in the dark about the family finances. As an optimist, I assume this too came from great intentions. The topic of money is considered "adult conversation," and we shouldn't burden or worry our kids with such adult speak.

I get it. Some conversations aren't meant for a child's ears. Kids don't need to carry the stress of not knowing whether or not you'll be able to pay the rent this month. They don't need to help you figure out how you're going to pay off mountains of debt. They didn't get you into debt, and they have no responsibility to get you out. But making the family finances a completely private matter is equally as devastating for your kids' financial future. Our children need to understand how personal finance works, and we—their parents—are the best teachers they have.

While nearly 73% of parents say they've talked to their teenagers about money management, 53% of teens say they want to learn more.[5] We think we're helping by keeping our finances private, but look at how many kids end up in the same financial heartache as their parents. Could we avoid this by letting our kids in on our mistakes? Probably. Kids are eager to learn, especially when it comes to money. If we're doing well financially, we need to show our kids what we're doing right. If we've messed up, we need to show our kids what we did wrong (and how we're fixing it). Let your kids learn from your mistakes. Trust me, they've already figured out you're not perfect. The idea that money is a taboo topic is causing continuous generations of financial failure.

Here's a real-world example. I'm active-duty military, and I've supervised plenty of young adults—18-year-old troops who are on their own for the first time. Many of these troops have never been grocery shopping alone before joining the military. How can they be expected to set a grocery budget if they aren't even sure how to shop for groceries? It's a real thing. I've taken them to the grocery store, immediately upon arrival to their first duty station, and often heard, "My mom usually does this. I'm not even sure what to buy." A few months later, these same kids are having difficulties making ends meet.

If we're willing to teach, our kids are willing to learn. If you don't think you're capable of teaching finances to your kids, the good news is, you can change your thinking. You *are* capable. That's why you're reading this book. First, *we must learn to talk about money*. In my research for writing this book, I've found this is more of an American issue than a global one, though it affects every country differently.

Tell Me About Your Finances

In the United States, it's offensive to ask someone their salary, or how much rent they pay, or how much they spent on their home. Many other countries don't have this social restriction. When I first moved to Italy, I had plenty of Italians ask how much money I earned, how much I pay in rent, and even how much it costs to raise five children. They also didn't mind sharing their info. I've noticed this same sentiment in other European countries and some Asian countries as well. It doesn't bother me, because I don't think finances should be as private as most people seem to think.

I'm a Christian, therefore, I have a biblical worldview. If you have a biblical worldview, you know it's all God's money anyway: your budget and mine. Why are we so afraid to talk about how much we have, or what we're doing with it? We can teach our kids to be discreet, but there are plenty of appropriate times to discuss money.

It seems like there are really only three reasons people don't like to talk about their personal finances:

1. **Parental Influence** – They were raised to not discuss money matters.
2. **Insecurity** – They are insecure about how much they make or how much they spend.
3. **Privacy** – They don't want others to know how much wealth or debt they've accumulated.

The first reason is merely a multi-generational misconception that money is yours, not God's, in the first place. If we humble ourselves and communicate, we could learn so much more from each other, which would eliminate our insecurities (i.e., the second reason). The third reason is understandable at times, as long as it doesn't stem from greed, so take caution. Talking about your finances in general doesn't mean you have to let the world know how much you have in the bank. I'm not suggesting you post your salary, and your monthly expenses, for the world to see, but I also wouldn't see a problem with it if you did. As far as income goes, that's exactly what the military does: they post it for everyone to see.

I know military members who won't tell you how much they

earn, and the funny thing is, they can't hide it. If you know someone's rank, and how long they've been in the service, you can look up their income on a current military pay chart, courtesy of Google. That shows how deeply ingrained this idea of fully privatizing our finances is in American culture. What if every career had public pay charts for everyone to see? I know more than a few people who would have serious problems with that, but why?

At minimum, open your finances up to your children to prepare them for adulthood.

Getting Your Children Involved

If you've hidden your finances from your kids in the past, start by showing them the family budget. If you don't have a family budget, there's never been a better time to start one, and you can bring your kids along for the ride. Before anything else, they need to understand how to manage their money. Otherwise, they're going from managing a few hundred bucks as a teen to managing a few thousand bucks a month as an adult, with no clue how to wisely save, invest, or spend any of it. Talk about a culture shock.

For younger children, when they ask for something in the store, don't just tell them "we can't afford it" or "it's not in the budget," show them the budget. By the way, you most likely *can* afford it, but you're choosing not to buy it, because of opportunity cost (we'll discuss this later). Let your kids see the monthly grocery or entertainment budget. Not only will it help them understand why you don't buy everything they ask for, it will help them prepare for their own grocery budget.

Show your kids the cost of things in your home. When

they're on the computer, show them the internet bill. If you have cable TV or a streaming service, show them how much you pay. Show them when you pay the rent, how you pay the rent, and how much rent you pay compared to others in your area. It can overwhelm your children to see all of this at once; it's easier for them to grasp, if you show them the costs along the way.

Start with these baby steps. Build your children up to managing their own household finances one day. When our kids ask why they can't have something, we turn the question back to them. This is how a typical conversation goes in the Bruce household:

> *Kid(s):* *"Can I have this thing that I can't live without, that I also didn't know existed until five minutes ago?" They don't actually say that last part.*
>
> *Us:* *"That's not in the budget, so we can't buy it today. Maybe you can save for it or put it on your wish list."*
>
> *Kid(s):* *"Why can't we just buy it, even if it's not in the budget?"*
>
> *Us:* *"That's a great question," that they know the answer to. "Why would we choose not to buy this thing?"*
>
> *Kid(s):* *"Because we're saving to pay cash for our house? And because if we buy this thing that means we can't buy something else?" We've had this conversation enough for them to know this is the case.*
>
> *Us:* *"That's exactly right. What's something else we spend a lot of money on?"*
>
> *Kid(s):* *"Traveling?"*

> **Us:** "Yes! And do you like to travel and see new places?" It's one of their favorite things.
>
> **Kid(s):** "Yes," they say, with a slightly disappointed, but understanding tone.
>
> **Us:** "Well that's why we can't spend our money on impulse buys and things that don't provide value to our lives. Plus, we want to be intentional with what we bring into our home, and impulse buys are the opposite of intentional."

This is a frequent conversation about money in our home. It's a moment to teach avoidance of impulse buys and to teach saving for short and long-term goals. They get it. They love to travel, and as a military family, we have the opportunity to travel around the world often. They understand financial trade-offs like this, but they have to be reminded. This is a great example of a teachable moment.

## Teachable Moments

You'll hear a lot about teachable moments throughout this book. Our kids know they can ask us financial questions, and we'll answer even the most personal ones. We don't shy away from the tough ones like how much we paid for our car, home, or any other big-ticket item. It's a teachable moment.

Every time your children have a money question, you can either shut them out, or bring them in, and use it as a teachable moment. In our experience, these moments are the best way to teach our kids. It's much easier to learn in the middle of a situation. Don't waste these moments; use them.

That being said, we do discourage our kids from talking

about the family finances with other kids. We don't want them bragging about how much money their parents spent on something and we discourage sharing other people's business in general. We want to make sure we use *our own* finances, and these *teachable moments*, as teaching tools for our kids. Try it. It's firsthand information. It's real. And they'll [usually] listen to you.

Money Isn't a Taboo Topic

I've had several couples ask for my financial help, and then back out when it came time to actually dive into their finances. Money can be a major stressor in marriage and bringing someone else in makes you feel vulnerable. I've been there. We had amassed $24,000 of consumer debt when my wife handed the finances over to me. She was stressed out and I wasn't helping. My spending was out of control, and I couldn't see it on paper since she was the one paying the bills. Once I actually saw how bad it was, I was too embarrassed to show the people who could help. I was in a situation many adults find themselves in: financially clueless and scared.

I had been raised on credit cards and bad financial decisions, and it showed. When I realized the severity of the situation, I knew I had to lead the way back to a healthy relationship with money. I wanted to know why some people were doing so well while so many others were making serious mistakes. Moreover, I wanted to join the United States Air Force, but our debt halted that too. That's when I got laser-focused on eliminating our debt. My wife and I both got extra jobs and continued working to pay off our debt over the next two years.

Now we're debt-free and I teach other people how to handle

their finances. If I can go from knowing nothing about money to being a good financial steward, you are more than capable of turning a bad financial situation around. I have read over 200 finance books that have completely changed my perspective on money. I took multiple financial courses, attended seminars, and completed a BA in Finance. I went from financial illiteracy to leaving a legacy. If you feel like a financial loser, it's a tough place to be. But for the sake of your family, you can't stay financially ignorant. You don't need a finance degree, and no, you don't need to read 200 finance books. It just takes a little learning.

You may feel inadequate to teach your kids about money, but you're fully capable. You may come from a history of financial mistakes, both personally and generationally, but that doesn't have to continue. We can equip our children to win with money, even if that means learning alongside them. It's easy to teach financial concepts to kids, because they're like little sponges. If you start early, you won't be helping them dig their way out of six-figure debt later.

Now for the big question: *How do you teach your kids about money if you don't know what you're doing?* It's easier than you think, but you have to start the process for yourself *now*. The basics of good finances are easy to learn. Things like:

- Don't spend more than you earn
- Invest simply, yet wisely
- Take advantage of compound interest
- Prepare for emergencies
- Avoid debt

This may seem like common sense, but these ideas aren't

commonly taught, nor are they commonly practiced. You don't have to be common. Being a good financial steward isn't common. It's good to be uncommon. You can be your family's change.

## You Can Be Your Family's Change

Does your family have a poor mindset? Ever heard of generational curses? There are choices made by previous generations that haunt us for decades. Break the generational chains of debt. Stop the generational addictions that kept your family poor. Whatever it is, it doesn't have to continue any longer. You can be the change you want to see in your family tree. Just like any other bad habit, poor financial skills can be fixed. The generational curse of poor finances can be broken. You can change everything. Start by learning good money management skills.

This book is going to cover many of the basics, and you have an endless supply of great finance books—starting with the reading list in the back of this book—to continue your education. If you're not much of a reader, consider audiobooks. I read over 50 books a year, which is only possible because of audiobooks. I found that my commute to work offered over an hour each day for self-education, and I took advantage of the time.

To save money, check with your local library. Money isn't an excuse to not know how to handle money. You can educate yourself for free. Why not start today? Well... I suppose that's the entire reason you're reading this book, so good on you.

---

We're about to get started on this journey to change your family for generations to come—to break generational financial curses. Before we do, I want to take a quick moment to explain why I started doing what I do.

I've been teaching families about money since 2013. I realized I was spending all my time helping people fix their money problems, instead of going to the root of the issue. That's when it hit me: the children are the roots.

There's a serious lack of financial education for our kids. Moreover, people are living unintentionally in almost every area of their lives. Many people look back and wonder what happened. It's time we, as parents, learn how to raise money-smart kids and lead intentional families.

I created FreedomSprout.com to fill a void. You can visit the website for countless resources to raise money-smart kids and live intentionally. I wrote this book to fill that same void. My wife and I have five kids, so we have the responsibility of getting five adults into the world with a solid knowledge of finances. We're not alone.

I think you understand the need for something like Freedom Sprout and for this book. Now let's get started.

Summary - Reframing Money

**Personal Finance Isn't Taught**
Since personal finance isn't taught in most schools, we have to accept the responsibility as parents to learn and teach our kids.

**We Don't Talk About Money**
We keep our children in the dark about the family finances. This leaves them knowing little about money when they leave the

house. We must let our children in on our financial life so they can prepare for theirs.

**Where We Can Involve Our Children**
We can use teachable moments to involve our children in our financial decisions. Teachable moments come up daily and provide an opportunity to show our children how to handle transactions and manage money.

**Be the Change in Your Family Tree**
Don't be afraid to talk about money. Become a student of finance and teach your children to do the same. If you've had success, show them how you've done it. If you've made mistakes, show them the mistakes and what you're doing to fix them.

## TWO
# TEACHING MONEY
### INSTILL A SENSE OF FINANCIAL SECURITY

"Kids don't remember what you try to teach them. They remember what you are."

JIM HENSON, CREATOR OF THE MUPPETS

"The best way to teach your kids about taxes is by eating 30% of their ice cream."

BILL MURRAY, ACTOR AND COMEDIAN

---

A YOUNG COUPLE CAME TO ME FOR FINANCE COACHING A FEW YEARS ago. They were doing pretty well, but worried they weren't doing everything they should be doing. I took a look at their finances and saw zero debt and almost $100,000 in a savings account. When I asked them what they were saving for, they said, "just whatever, I guess; we want to make sure we have money in case anything happens."

They had a $100,000 emergency fund. For a couple that doesn't make $100,000 in a year, combined, this was a little overkill. And by a little, I mean it was probably $90,000 more than they truly needed for an emergency fund. Especially since they had extremely secure jobs with the military.

Why did they amass so much money and put it in a savings account bearing practically no interest? Because they were afraid. They were financially insecure. On paper, they were doing great, but in their minds, they were never going to have enough. They were always worried about losing the money if they invested it, and afraid to make any large purchases, like a home, even though they could have paid cash for a small starter home in that part of the country.

That's a common story. It's financial incompetence, but it's also financial insecurity at its best. Or worst, rather. This couple wasn't financially insecure in the sense most people think of when they hear the word *insecure*. Financial insecurity has little to do with how much money you have and much more to do with how you view money. They had plenty of money for their lifestyle, but they would have likely been insecure with any amount higher. It wasn't about having a certain amount. They were insecure about managing their finances because they both grew up poor. There are lots of reasons people are financially insecure, as you'll see at the end of this chapter. So much of that has to do with a person's upbringing. Don't freak out. You're not going to "ruin" your kids. With a few easy-to-implement ideas, you can find ways to instill a healthy view of money in your children. You won't have to worry about your kids being financially insecure. It starts through making daily lessons from things we all do regularly.

## How to Teach Kids About Money

When it comes to teaching children about money, we've established that most parents feel inadequate. It's hard to feel qualified when you aren't doing great with your own money, but you can do this.

To begin the process of teaching a subject outside of your expertise, you will need books, videos, online courses, and a lot of time. I've done the majority of the leg work for you in this book. Now, you can get to work learning for yourself so you can, in turn, teach your children!

Go through the process. If you're not good with money, admit it. Accept it. Then change it. You don't need a masters degree in Economics to get started. Let them learn with you. With technology, we have so many resources. Let's take advantage of those resources.

All of life is a learning experience. Teach your kids throughout life, and teach them the value of lifelong learning. Any time the opportunity presents itself to show your child how you did something smart with money, or made a financial mistake, use it to teach. If you're not sure what to do in a situation, pull out your phone and do a quick search to understand what you need to do. Seriously, Google it. There's no shame in that.

You'll find that many of the places you go in your daily life offer teachable moments. Here are a few of the most common:

- **At the Bank** – Explain the process of taking money out of the bank and depositing money. Make sure they understand it's all *your* earned money; the bank isn't a magic-money machine.
- **At the Store** – What better place to teach the basic concepts of budgeting than at the store? Let your kids see how you keep a list and stick to it, and how that keeps you within your budget.
- **At Expensive Places** – Amusements parks, heavy tourist destinations, and carnivals all have one thing in common: they're crazy expensive. Show your kids how these places may not be the best place to stretch their dollars, but also show them it's ok to trade money for life experiences.

Dave Ramsey's daughter, Rachel Cruze, likes to say, "more is caught than taught." Your kids will see what you do before they'll hear what you say. Model good financial principles for them. Don't pretend you're rich in front of your kids. Explain to your kids if you have struggled with managing money. Show them how you want them to have a better start than you had. Once you get that out of the way, learn with them.

Make it fun. You can use financial toys to teach life concepts. This is especially true for younger kids. You've got piggy banks, toy checkbooks, toy cash registers, and play money. Kids love toys and kids love learning about money. It's a great combination.

Other than hands-on toys, there are games to teach your kids about money. Younger children prefer learning through play, but as they age they will want more challenging games. It's easy to say something like, "let's play this game as a family so you guys can be millionaires one day." What kid can pass that offer up? On FreedomSprout.com, there's a list of over 50 board games and card games to teach your kids about money (just do a search for "games").

You have so many resources at your fingertips. Use them! When you add all these methods together, your kids will succeed financially. As your kids continue to age, you can add in more complex topics— especially in the teenage years.

Teaching Teens About Money

If you haven't taught your teen anything about money, there's still plenty of time. Simply give them a good financial foundation before they leave home. Now is the time to squash any myths your teen believes and start planting the seeds of true financial freedom.

Teach your teens gradually with teachable moments. Show them the things you do daily. Things you may not typically think to teach your teen. Here are some examples:

- How to use an ATM
- How to count change
- How to calculate a tip
- How to check in at a hotel
- How rent and deposits work
- How to pay a utility bill
- How to rent a car
- How to write a check (yes, we still need to know this)

As your children approach their early teens, let them see you do all of these things. Walk them through the process as you do it. Having worked in customer service for years, I was surprised by how many kids don't know how to pay for food at a restaurant. And counting change seems to be a lost art. We take the things we do every day for granted, because we've been doing them for so long. Your children may have never done any of these things. It's our responsibility to be their guides.

Opening a checking account for your teen is a great way to help them understand money management. Saving for a car is a great way to teach delayed gratification, so a savings account is also a good idea. There are many ways to raise financially responsible teens, and it all begins with giving them a little control. We'll talk more about specific accounts your kids should understand in the coming pages.

By now, they should be spending their own money, and not asking mom and dad for a handout every time they want to buy something. They're ready to create their first budget, even if it only includes a few things. It will be easier to show them how to track a small budget as they enter adulthood than dealing with an overwhelmed 25-year-old with countless bills to pay and no budget. Your teen will be looking for a job, if they don't already have one. A strong work ethic is something to be instilled by the parents, through the job your child accepts.

The "debt talk" is one of the most important talks you can have with your teen. Explain the dangers of debt, and how it's always best to avoid it. Go over all the ways your teen can go to college without getting into debt, which we'll cover in Chapter 8. Their friends may be acquiring student loans at the same rate as they acquire friends on social media, but your children will know better.

Generosity is another lesson to be taught early, and it will become even more important in the teenage years. Famous

Holocaust victim, Anne Frank, said, "No one has ever become poor by giving." Giving is taught. The importance of being generous has to be instilled in your child. From tipping a server to giving to major charitable projects, giving and sharing is part of life, and an important part. "Give and you shall receive," is a true statement, but giving for the sake of giving, and to get nothing in return, is important to grasp.

Continue to teach your teens about tithing, or rather, generous giving in general, beyond merely giving 10%.[1] Teach them that no dollar given is ever regretted. Generosity isn't just about supporting your church or feeding the homeless. It can be so much more than that. There are countless causes in need of money. Sure, you can always give your time and services, and you should, but sometimes the cause just needs money. If your child only gets one lesson before leaving home, let it be the lesson of generosity.

Financial insecurity is one thing that can lead to the "I don't have enough money to give" mindset. Before we get into all the things we need to teach our kids about, let's talk about financially insecurity.

What Keeps Us Financially Insecure

We have a serious problem. Thirty-eight percent of U.S. households have credit card debt and 43% of people with student loans aren't making payments.[2] We can do better and the next generation can surpass our generation in financial literacy. Honestly, it wouldn't be hard.

What's making everyone so financially insecure? How can we keep that from being passed on to the next generation? We aren't trying to make our kids filthy rich, but we want them to be financially secure. Money shouldn't be a major stressor for our kids, and it doesn't have to be. What does financial insecurity look like? Let's look a little closer.

I'm going to close this chapter with the eight things keeping people financially insecure. Before we get into the weeds in the rest of the book, we need to face the insecurities that keep people struggling.

**1. A Financially Insecure Childhood**

I've met more than a few millionaires who don't feel financially secure because of the environment they grew up in. Growing up under conditions where basic needs are not being met cuts deep into the heart of a person. It is a trauma that can haunt them for a lifetime, no matter how much money they make.

People who lived during The Great Depression still have habits that were ingrained in them during those years of deprivation. If you grew up poor, you still have habits you took with you from your childhood. Some of these habits are helpful (e.g., frugality, planning, budgeting), and others are harmful (e.g., hoarding, greed, insecurity). Despite your situation as a child, there is hope!

How do you battle the financially insecure childhood you had? Well, goals help a lot. When you can see you're on the right track to live a financially secure life, it helps you breathe a little easier. When you have a goal set, you have something to reach for, and you'll know when you get there. If you don't have a plan, you'll stay financially insecure.

**2. Not Being Financially Literate**

Two-thirds of American adults can't pass a basic financial literacy test.[3] That shouldn't come as a surprise since we already established that finance isn't taught in schools.

How do you battle financial illiteracy? Start by taking the time to learn how money really works, and then pass that down to your kids. Teach your kids about money. Teach them finance terms. Teach them to invest. Teach them to budget. Teach them everything you're about to learn.

## 3. Not Controlling Your Money

Financial illiteracy leads to out-of-control spending, and a lack of clear direction for your money. Around one-third of Americans actually keep a budget.[4] If you don't have control over your money and how you want to allocate it, it will never matter how much you make. When you earn $5 million per year, and spend $6 million, you're still broke. The amount you make isn't the issue. Knowing where your money goes is the issue.

How do you control your money? Simple: a budget. There's freedom in a budget. A budget allows you to get the most out of every dollar you earn.

## 4. Not Having a Plan

One-third (seems like a common statistic) of U.S. adults have saved absolutely nothing for retirement so far, and less than 50% have over $10,000 in savings.[5] People aren't ready for retirement, and most don't even have a plan for it. How can you reach a goal you don't have? Financial security comes from a financial blueprint and a financial blueprint only comes from doing the work of making a plan.

How do you battle not having a plan? You create the plan that works for you. If you're not comfortable making your own plan, you might consider a fee-only financial advisor to help navigate the unknown of investment planning. Fee-only financial advisors tend to have your best interest in mind, because they make the same amount of money no matter which plan they suggest. If your kids have a plan early on, they won't have to worry. Saving and investing small amounts, from a young age, could be all the plan your children need.

**5. Not Understanding How Debt Works**

U.S. consumer debt is over $4 trillion, with credit card debt making up one-fourth of that.[6] The American public needs to realize the minimum payment is a joke. We're acting like children with Monopoly money and no real sense of responsibility for our own future. When we amass mountains of credit card debt, it weighs on us and makes financial security impossible. Often, the parents' debt starts the process for the child to become financially insecure. Debt is the root of most financial problems... especially financial insecurity.

How do you battle the debt problem? The easiest way is to never start accumulating it. If you do use credit cards, pay them off, in full, every month. If you can't, don't use credit cards. Debit cards are a great alternative if your credit spending is out of control.

**6. Not Having Adequate Insurance**

In 2017, close to 30 million Americans didn't have health insurance.[7] The numbers haven't changed much. Insurance is a trillion-dollar industry, and there are thousands of insurance companies across the United States.[8] Yet, so many Americans don't have enough insurance, and even worse, they don't understand most insurance policies. It's important to have the right amount of coverage but understanding what you're buying is just as important.

How do you battle insurance illiteracy? If you can't afford to replace it, insure it. We'll talk more about how insurance works shortly. Adequate insurance is part of a bigger financial picture.

**7. Not Seeing the Bigger Picture**

Life isn't just working to survive; we should thrive. Are we just working to pay bills or to have a nice house? Do we want to leave a legacy for our children? We need to have a long-term perspective that aligns our finances with our values.

How do you see the bigger picture? Take a step back and evaluate your financial situation. Set some goals and determine where you want to be in five, ten, or twenty years. Spend time thinking about what is important to you and where you really want to be in life, while also being thankful for where you are now and what you have today.

**8. Not Being Grateful**

We're all guilty of being ungrateful at times, but did you know it will keep you financially insecure? If you always seek more, you'll never appreciate what you have. You'll never have enough.

How do you become grateful? Practice gratitude by starting small. List three things you're grateful for every morning. It won't be hard to find those things, and if it is, you may want to look at your mindset. Teach your kids to be grateful and thankful. If you teach it from the start, they won't feel financially insecure later. Teach your kids to list three things each morning. These little habits actually work.

Summary - Teaching Money

**How to Teach Children About Money**
Teachable moments come up every day. Places like banks, grocery stores, and tourist traps all provide an opportunity for children to learn about money in one way or another.
Finance books, games, and toys will help you and your children learn while having fun.

**Teaching Teens About Money**
It's never too early to start, but if your children are in their teens, you need to start now.

Show your teens how to make basic daily financial transactions you may not even think about. Making purchases and paying bills are natural parts of life, but often we've been doing them so long, we don't think about teaching them to our teens.

Have the "debt talk" with your teens as soon as possible.
Instill a love of giving in your children.

**Things That Keep Us Financially Insecure**
Financial insecurity causes many of our financial problems.

Identifying and facing the eight pitfalls of financial insecurity will help us raise financially secure children:

1. Correct the habits learned from a financially insecure childhood.
2. Become financially literate.
3. Gain control of your money.
4. Develop a plan.
5. Understand how debt works.
6. Know how to purchase insurance.
7. Focus on the bigger picture.
8. Remember to be grateful.

# THREE
# MONEY LESSONS
### PREPARE YOUR KIDS FOR ADULTHOOD

"We may not be able to prepare the future for our children, but we can at least prepare our children for the future."

FRANKLIN D. ROOSEVELT, 32ND PRESIDENT OF THE UNITED STATES

"Money doesn't change men, it merely unmasks them. If a man is naturally selfish or arrogant or greedy, the money brings that out, that's all."

HENRY FORD, FOUNDER OF THE FORD MOTOR COMPANY

"If I tell the kids I can't buy them something the standard response is, 'Just use the card,' so clearly they're set up for financial success."

VALERIE (VALEEGRRL), DEPUTY NEWS EDITOR OF<br>SCARY MOMMY

---

WITHIN SIX MONTHS OF OUR WEDDING, MY WIFE AND I GOT A LETTER from a company inviting us to join their wholesale club. It seemed like a good deal, so we went to see what it was all about. When we arrived, they gave a brilliant presentation and made it seem like everything we ever bought would be cheaper if we bought it from this club—and they really made it seem like they sold *everything*.

We were waiting on the $500 price tag, or perhaps $1,000. Of course, they never mentioned the price in the presentation. After they finished up, we had to make a decision to join the club or not. I mean that literally: we *had* to make a decision. They told us we only had one chance.

If we walked out, we would *never* be able to join their club.

That was the day we learned the importance of sleeping on big financial decisions. It's a great first money lesson for your kids: *never make a large purchase without sleeping on it*. We learned this the painful way; your child doesn't have to. "Sleeping on it" could literally mean waiting overnight, but the important takeaway is to take the necessary time to think about big financial decisions. I prefer actually taking the night to do so.

The price of this wholesale club wasn't $500 or $1,000; the price tag was almost $4,000. Due to the fear of missing out

(FOMO), we joined the club. Over the next few years, we bought a baby crib. That's it. We couldn't seem to find the great prices on other things like they showed us in the presentation. We got played.

If we had just known to sleep on big decisions, we wouldn't have spent $4,000 on a $200 crib. If only we had understood marketing tactics like, "you must make a decision now," and how those tactics are used when someone is selling a product people wouldn't buy if they had time to think on it, we wouldn't have lost that $4,000.

That's just one example of what you'll be able to teach your kids before they leave home. Your kids will be prepared for any major financial decision, and they'll know how to approach it. There are so many basic life skills kids need before they leave home. It's not the responsibility of anyone else, including the school system, to teach our kids these skills.

We want to spare our kids some of the heartache from our past mistakes and that's why we want to teach them these truths. We'll get into some more concepts and lessons soon, but let's start with a list of things your kids absolutely must know before moving out on their own. We can implement many of these ideas during teachable moments throughout each day. We can implement the more complex ideas by sitting down and having a conversation with our kids.

## 9 Things to Know Before Leaving Home

### 1. How to Open and Manage Accounts

Young adults need their own checking accounts to be able to

manage their income and pay their bills when they're on their own. Your kids must understand how to open a checking account, whether online or at the bank, and how to keep enough money in the account. Whether you go into your local bank or open online accounts, walk them through the process.

Teach your kids to have a buffer in the account. For example, if you have a $200 buffer in your checking, then $200 is your new zero. When you get close to that mark, deposit more money so it doesn't go below $200. This keeps padding for unexpected expenses, fees, or accidental overspending, and it can serve as a mini-emergency fund.

A savings account is next. This is just as easy to open but pay attention to any fees for pulling money out too often, as well as potential annual fees, and a required minimum amount that may need to be in the account.

Managing those accounts is the important part. Keeping enough money in them, tracking expenses to avoid overdraft fees, and monitoring expenses to avoid fraudulent charges are all key points for your children to understand.

**2. The Importance of Giving**

Whether you believe in the Bible when it says giving "rebukes the devourer" (Malachi 3:11), or if you simply believe in helping others, giving is vital to your finances. When my wife and I started a regular routine of giving, we began to see the supernatural happen in our lives. There were changes in our finances we never thought possible.

Other than what the Bible says and my personal experience, giving increases happiness. Studies show that your brain associates giving with pleasure and reward.[1] People who give are happier in general than people who don't. Giving is actually increasing and becoming more popular.[2] Perhaps more people are learning that it really is better to give than to receive.

## 3. How to Be a Savvy Shopper

If you're frugal, you likely do things you don't even realize you do when you shop. We must teach our kids these things. You can't expect them to automatically know how you shop, and *why* you shop that way.

The single biggest way to save money when shopping—and in life in general—is to not base your purchases on what other people think. This goes for anything, from what you eat to what you drive. You probably know this concept as "keeping up with the Joneses." If you haven't heard, the Joneses may look rich, but they're broke. How many people do you know who have a lot of expensive stuff, but not a lot of money? We should teach our kids to distinguish between *being* wealthy and *looking* wealthy.

If you don't consider yourself a savvy shopper, here's a quick breakdown of the basics:

- **Plan your meals ahead of time.** If you plan your weekly menu, you can buy exactly what you need. This prevents impulse buys and unnecessary groceries. Remember when we talked about your kids seeing you stick to a list?
- **Plan around sales.** Living your entire life eating unhealthy foods—simply because they are cheaper—is not a good way to live. Supermarkets put food on sale too often for you to be eating cheap, nasty food, day after day.

- **Buy in bulk when it makes sense.** Buying in bulk is not always the best option, but for things you know you'll need and that don't expire (e.g., paper products, cleaning products, etc.), bulk is a good option.
- **Use coupons, but don't go overboard.** Don't spend five hours clipping coupons to save $10—that's not worth your time. However, a quick skimming of the weekly coupons for items already on your list is worth it. Look for in-store coupons as well as online coupons. A study from the marketing firm Valassis showed almost 70% of people will switch from their favorite brand based on a coupon.[3] So much for brand loyalty, but it shows there isn't as much difference between products as people like to believe. Don't let coupons completely change your behavior, as studies show they do,[4] but let them be an addition to your savings tools.

These are just a few simple ideas, but over a lifetime, they can save you and your children a fortune.

### 4. Debt Can Ruin Your Life

Debt is often the first topic in any finance book or course. Why? Because it's the single largest contributing factor to keeping people poor (often through auto loans, but we'll talk about this later). According to the Federal Reserve, the majority of U.S. citizens have installment loans, and an astounding 44% of Americans have revolving credit card balances (balances that aren't paid off each month).[5] I suspect it's actually much higher.

The sad thing is, this is normal.

U.S. consumers owe $927 billion in credit card debt alone—that's a $15,000 average per household, according to a study by NerdWallet.[6] However, in a recent study by Ramsey Solutions, the *total* consumer debt is more than double that figure per household, at $34,055.[7] What's the cause of all that debt? Often, it is emergencies. Establishing an emergency fund will drastically reduce the chances of your child falling into this pit of debt. You don't want your kids to fall into the debt trap. We'll talk more about emergency funds in Chapter 5.

Debt really can ruin your life. It happens every day. Your kids need to know the destructive powers of debt before they get their first credit card offer.

**5. Credit Isn't That Important**

Plenty of finance gurus and bloggers will tell you obtaining a high credit score is an important first step for your child. In reality, it may not be as important as you think, unless your kids want to live a life of debt. And if they do want that, please refer them back to point #5. If you're teaching your kids to stay out of debt, a credit score isn't so important. Your children will still be able to get a mortgage later on—if they choose to do so—through a process called manual underwriting. The Balance published a detailed article on the process of manual underwriting. Here's what they had to say about it:

> *"The key to high credit scores is a history of borrowing and repaying loans. But some people choose to live without debt, which can bring simplicity and significant interest savings. Unfortunately, your credit eventually evaporates along with your interest costs. You don't necessarily have bad credit—you have no credit profile at all (good or*

bad). Still, it's possible to get a loan with no FICO score if you go through manual underwriting. In fact, having no credit or thin credit can be better than numerous negative items (like bankruptcy or collections) in your credit reports." [8]

If you're thinking these sound like hurdles that could be avoided with a credit score, consider the other possibility of what could happen if building a credit score goes wrong: your child could get trapped in mountains of debt. You can help your kids to avoid making decisions purely to build their credit score.

Once they're responsible, if they want credit so badly, it's easy to build it over time by using credit cards and having them set to automatically be paid off, in full, every single month. They can start with secured credit cards (cards that require a security deposit, mostly used specifically for building credit) and work their way up to standard credit cards with no annual fees and good rewards. But again, this shouldn't be done just to build a credit score. Especially if they don't plan to need one. We'll talk more about how unimportant credit scores really are in Chapter 7.

### 6. Budgets Give You Freedom

The word "budget" is an ugly word to many. It sounds boring. Budgets aren't sexy, nor are they a "necessary evil." Budgets are freeing. Once you get comfortable with a budget, it can actually be fun to stretch your money.

For example, a "fun money" category shows your kids how budgets can be exciting. You can allocate a certain amount to spend on anything you want for that month, and not feel guilty about it, if it's in your "fun money" category. If your kid isn't into writing and numbers, paper budgets may steer them away from wanting to learn about budgeting. Technology will win over the majority of kids.

There are so many tools out today, like EveryDollar, Mint, and Personal Capital.[9] These tools make budgeting easy, fun, and often automatic. There are a thousand other possible tools to use. Find what works for you and your children.

## 7. Automation is Powerful

There is no need, with technology today, to pay all your bills manually. You can automate investing, saving, utilities, monthly bills, and even giving. When you automate everything you can, you're left with a small amount to budget each month. You can even automate budgeting to an extent with the tools we discussed earlier, by connecting your accounts and having the categories sorted automatically for each expense. Automate your own finances, and then show your kids how to do the same with theirs. It only takes a few minutes.

In *The Automatic Millionaire: A Powerful One-Step Plan to Live and Finish Rich*, David Bach explains the power of automation:[10]

> "You don't need a budget
>   You don't need willpower
>   You don't need to make a lot of money
>   You don't need to be that interested in money
>   You can set up the plan [to automate your finances] in an hour. You can take the time, in the beginning, to set your finances on a system of automation. That leaves you focusing on a small percentage to actually make the spending decisions."

## 8. How to Nail a Job Interview

What's the secret to a great job interview? Understanding how to interact with people well. If your children can interact well, they can nail a job interview.

A good interview needs basic things like a firm handshake, eye contact, confidence, and honest conversation, but that isn't just for job interviews. Instead of merely giving your kids a few common points for a good job interview, I suggest you teach your kids how to generally interact with people in an authentic way.

There are plenty of books on dealing with people that should be required reading in college, if not high school. Refer to the reading list in the back of this book for some great recommendations this topic. If your kids are comfortable with people and know how to interact well with them, a job interview will be easy.

## 9. How Insurance Works

When children leave home, they may still be under your insurance in some areas, but it's important that they know how to plan for several different types of insurance.

Here are the basics your kids will need to know about immediately:

- **Health Insurance** – Check your family insurance and see when it runs out for your children. Some policies go until they are 25, even if they're married. I suggest helping your children find their own health insurance when the time comes. It's important they get a

reasonable price, while also receiving good coverage. Many employers will cover health insurance, but it depends on the type of job. Part-time jobs often provide no coverage.
- **Car Insurance** – Your children will need to understand the difference between full coverage and liability. Get them to look for a quality insurance company. Odds are, the cheapest company won't provide the best coverage and service.
- **Rental Insurance** – Before your children buy their own home, they'll likely be renting a house or apartment. Insuring the contents of that home is important, and it's typically quite affordable.

And later on (but not much later):

- **Home Insurance** – Your children may not be immediately moving into a mortgage, but if and when they decide to buy a home, they need to know what to look for. Teach them to read the fine print to see what's covered. Many insurance policies don't cover things like burglary, house fires, or destruction during a time of war (yes, this is actually outlined in policies).
- **Life Insurance** – Life insurance is for the people survived by you; it's not for *you*. If your children don't have a family of their own yet, they don't need to worry about life insurance right away, other than possibly burial costs. But down the road, and before they are old enough to start seeing a dramatic increase in rates, they will need life insurance. Once the time comes, go for term life insurance over whole life

insurance. Term insurance is a more affordable option, and when people do their research, it seems to be the majority preference. Many companies offer cashback-term policies now, which means at the end of your term, you can receive up to a 100% refund on the money you paid for the policy, given you don't die.
- **Disability Insurance** – This can be important from an early age, but it's not always necessary as soon as your children move out. Make sure they understand what disability insurance is, and they have a plan to get it, should they ever need it.

Young adults often look for the cheapest version of any insurance, without considering the coverage. Quality is important, but insurance premiums shouldn't bankrupt your child. There's a balance. Most other insurance outside of what's mentioned above is either unnecessary, a scam, or only required for specific situations.

The only other type of insurance you may want to consider is identity-theft protection. There's nothing identity-theft protection companies do that you can't do yourself, but it will save you loads of time and headaches in the event you ever become a victim.

Now let's go through some important terms and concepts your kids need to know.

## 9 Concepts to Understand

Oxford's Dictionary of Finance and Banking isn't the best birthday present for a toddler, but you can incorporate a few important finance concepts at a young age. New money terms can be introduced periodically. Teach kids words they can understand in a context they can grasp.

Children learn better with hands-on experiences in science,[11] which directly correlates to the social science of economics… well, to money in general, really. We've already discussed some important terms, like budget, debt, checking accounts, insurance, and savings accounts. There are a few more concepts and ideas they need to know so we can build on them throughout the book.

**1. Compound Interest**

This may be the most important term in this book. That's why the power of it was listed in the previous section, and you'll hear it several more times. Children must understand compound interest as soon as possible. It's important for them to know:

1. **How it works for them:** Investing from a young age can turn a little into a whole lot. $100 invested at 10% interest (annually) means you will have $110 next year. That means $110 at 10% will turn into $121 the following year, and on and on. We'll come back to this later to make sure you understand it. Look out for a pop quiz!
2. **How it works against them:** A credit card charging a 24% APR (Annual Percentage Rate) will render your minimum payment useless over time. A $150 payment on a $5,000 balance will cost you over $3,000 in interest and take almost five years to pay off.

Around 40% of adults don't understand the power of compound interest. We don't want our kids to be one of those adults.[12]

If your children start young, invest simply, and let compound interest do the work, their retirement will be just fine. We'll dive deeper into investing in Chapter 9; for now, just know it's important to start early, because of compound interest.

## 2. Diversification

Diversification means having a Plan A, B, C, etc., and this is something you can explain from an early age. Teach your kids to be prepared for anything, regardless of whether something appears to be a good deal.

Show young children how they can diversify with their crayons. For example, a box of eight crayons will give you a few options for coloring, but a box of 120 crayons will give you endless options. A larger box of crayons also accounts for the unforeseen: the occasional broken crayon. It's a great analogy and teaching tool.

True diversity in investing means investing in stocks, bonds, cash, real estate, commodities, and endless other options. There's also diversity within the diversity. Within stocks alone, you have options for U.S. stocks, international, tech companies, oil companies, and the list goes on. The key lesson here is for your children to understand the importance of not putting all their eggs in one basket. You can even literally use eggs and a basket to explain the concept of diversifying investments, if your kids are visual learners.

## 3. Dollar-Cost Averaging

Dollar-cost averaging is an investment method where you invest a fixed dollar amount (typically into a mutual fund—we're about to talk about these), on a set schedule, regardless of the share price. This means you'll buy more stocks and/or bonds when the share price is lower, and less when the share price is higher.

While this is an extremely simple concept, it's teaching your child a bigger lesson: "playing" the stock market is a loser's game. The average person cannot pick winning stocks. The average person cannot successfully "buy low and sell high," outside of dollar-cost averaging. Most famous investors are known for their hectic, busy schedules of spending up to 120 hours a week doing research and making investments. That's not my idea of a fulfilling life, but it's your call, and it will be your children's call as well… but let's get back to dollar-cost averaging.

You can teach dollar-cost averaging to your children by letting them put a certain amount of money into a savings account every month. It should be the same amount each time, and on the same day of the month. And teach the "why" behind doing this, since a savings account doesn't have a fluctuating share price, and it won't gain much interest. You're merely building the dollar-cost averaging habit.

**Note:** The idea of dollar-cost averaging is still often tied to lump-sum investing (i.e., investing a large sum of money you suddenly acquired). When used in this sense, it's typically just called DCA. Here I am referring to dollar-cost averaging as an everyday investing method. Dollar-cost averaging may not be the most appropriate strategy for investing a lump sum. See a fee-only financial advisor if you need to make that decision.

## 4. Inflation

My parents often said things like, "when I was a kid, you could buy a pack of gum for a dime." Younger kids will ask why—don't lose the teachable moment. If you talk about how things used to be cheaper, and don't use it as a lesson, you're really just complaining. That's not a trait you want to pass down to your kids.

Your children need to grasp the concept of inflation, and the fact that it isn't going anywhere but up. They also need to understand how wages rise with inflation so they're not afraid of everything costing more than they can afford. A healthy understanding (not fear) of inflation, is all your kids need. Google some charts that show prices and average incomes 10 years ago, and 20, and 30… you get the idea.

## 5. Mutual Fund

Once your children are old enough to understand the basic concept of the stock market, it's time to explain mutual funds. Plain and simple, a mutual fund is a group of stocks from various companies that make up one fund. This allows you to own part of anywhere from 20 companies to thousands of companies, depending on the fund you buy. It's instant diversity within the stock market.

Before your children actually buy a mutual fund, they need to be able to understand and, more importantly, know the difference between actively managed funds and passively managed funds:

- **Actively Managed Funds** – A fund manager selects the stocks, based on his or her own research. If the fund manager isn't good at picking stocks, your mutual fund will suffer. Since we've already established people's ability to pick winning stocks, or lack thereof, active funds aren't usually as successful as passive funds.
- **Passively Managed Funds** – These are also referred to as index funds. These funds are computer-generated, based on a specific index. The Dow Jones, S&P 500, and the NASDAQ are all indexes, and you can buy an index fund based on any one of them. Passively managed funds are usually the better option for a number of reasons. Let's talk more about those reasons…

Out of the hundreds of books I've read about investing, the primary theme in almost all of them is to invest in passively managed funds (index funds). Passive funds outperform active funds the majority of the time. Morningstar, a global financial services firm, did the research and found, "only 23% of all active funds surpassed the average of their passive rivals over the 10-year period, which ended in June of 2019."[13] And if you're getting excited about the funds within that 23%, it's important to know, it's never the same funds that outperform their passive counterparts.

## 6. Net Worth

Ask most kids if they want to be a millionaire and you will get a unanimous "yes!". Most children have no idea what being a millionaire entails, but they know it will allow them to buy anything they want, including rocketships, private islands, pirate boats, and possibly their own country. Sure, kids may overestimate what $1 million will actually buy them, but you have their attention at "million."

This is where net worth comes in, because that's how you know if you're a millionaire or not. Being a millionaire doesn't mean having a stack of 10,000 hundred-dollar bills buried under the concrete in your basement though, technically, that does make you a millionaire. Being a millionaire means having a net worth of at least $1 million, and rarely is all of that in cash. So now I'm going to add a couple more terms for your kids to know:

1. **Asset** – Anything that has value and/or appreciates in value and doesn't depreciate.
2. **Liability** – Anything that costs you money to own or depreciates in value.

In short: assets make money; liabilities lose money. *Net worth is calculated by subtracting your liabilities from your assets.*

### Assets – Liabilities = Net Worth

You can use the cost of your home to show your children how this works. If your home appraises for $200,000, and you owe the bank $100,000, you would have a net worth of $100,000 (again, taking only your home into account). As they grasp the concept of *assets – liabilities = net worth*, you can add your investments, vehicles, loans, etc., to find your true net worth. This method helps them see how debt takes a chunk out of your increasing wealth. Your children's ultimate financial goal should be to increase their net worth. Increasing assets means increasing wealth.

**7. Opportunity Cost**

Any time you buy something, you're sacrificing the ability to spend that money on something else. That's called opportunity cost. It's the cost of what you *can't do* with that money, because of what *you are doing* with it. And the same applies to time. This concept helps you to evaluate your choices when you have a limited resource like time or money.

It's easy to find real-life examples of opportunity cost. The next time your children want to spend their own money on a video game, explain the many things they can't spend their money on if they choose to spend it on the game, including the lost ability to put it into savings, which will increase in value, versus on the game which will probably lose value.

This shows kids that everything in life is a tradeoff, and it helps them make an informed decision when spending money. Just make sure they don't get too serious about it and hoard all of their money, fearing to ever spend it on anything.

**8. Rule of 72**

The *Rule of 72* tells you how many years it will take an investment to double in size, based on the size of the investment and the interest rate. It's easy to calculate: 72, divided by the annual ROR (rate of return), equals the years it will take for your investment to double:

**72/ROR = Years to Double**

As long as you have a fixed, annual return, this formula works. It's not accurate to the penny, and it wouldn't be used for making serious financial calculations, but that's not its purpose. The purpose of the *Rule of 72* is to give you a ballpark estimate on an investment decision. You would then get specific on the numbers if it looks appealing.

**9. Tax**

Explain the different types of taxes, such as income tax, sales tax, specific tax on specific items, and certain taxes that apply to certain states. Young children have the ability to understand how and why we pay taxes. The world they enjoy is full of things that have been built with tax money (e.g., roads, bridges, and buildings). It doesn't have to turn into a political conversation, as long as they understand when and why we pay taxes.

These nine concepts are only a fraction of what your kids need to know. Teach these ideas as soon as the opportunity presents itself. For more finance terms, refer to the Kid's Finance Glossary on FreedomSprout.com—simply do a search for "glossary".

Finance is more than numbers and figures. Responding appropriately when finance decisions need to be made is a behavioral science. It's a mindset. Wisdom plays as much, if not more, of a role than knowledge in making financial decisions.

## 7 Pieces of Money Wisdom

Have you ever learned something new and thought, *the rest of the world probably knew this for most of their lives, and I was today-years-old when I figured it out*? We all have, because there's a lot to learn. We cannot possibly know everything there is to know and some things will inevitably slip through the cracks.

Since we can't turn back time, we can do the next best thing: teach our children the things we wish we had learned at a young age. Below, I've compiled some of the best money wisdom I've learned that doesn't seem to be common knowledge—the things I wish I had known earlier. Things that will make your kids wealthy in every sense of the word.

### 1. Mindset is the Key

The primary difference between the wealthy and those who are struggling financially is mindset. The second half of this book is entirely devoted to mindset, because I believe it to be that important on the road to financial freedom and a fulfilled life.

Full disclaimer: Before we go on, my purpose is not to make this the "rich vs. poor" argument, nor am I saying that people in either situation are there simply based on mindset. But mindset is one of the most important pieces to life's puzzle.

Talk to people in different socio-economic classes, and you'll see how true this is. Most often, it comes down to accepting responsibility. If someone is willing to accept the fact that, regardless of the cards they were dealt, they are the only one who can change their finances, then they can start to do something about it. It's hard to do anything about it if you're waiting on someone else to do it for you, or if you just choose to complain instead of act. Where you are in life is not always your *fault*, but it is always your *responsibility* to change it. It's not anyone else's responsibility.

Change comes by working on your own finances and teaching your children how to have a financially secure future. You have to start where you are, without blaming anyone else, because blaming others for financial problems isn't helpful for anyone.

Our society has a big issue with entitlement right now. It starts early in the lives of our children, from the first "that's not fair," but proper guidance reverses the effects of entitlement. We'll talk more about entitlement later.

## 2. Buy Assets, Not Liabilities

We touched on "assets vs. liabilities" in the net worth section, but it deserves more attention. Wealthy people buy assets and poor people buy liabilities. If you spend your life primarily buying assets, and minimizing liabilities, you'll become wealthy by default. If you get your kids into the mindset of focusing on assets over liabilities, half the battle for their financial success is already won. Assets and liabilities don't keep track of themselves; that's personal responsibility. That's why you measure your wealth.

## 3. Measure by Net Worth

Your wealth isn't measured purely by the size of your bank account. Your wealth is measured by your net worth. Never measure by how much stuff you have or how nice your car is;

you're basically going backwards at that point. The only true measurement of financial wealth is net worth.

**Note:** I know it may seem like my ultimate goal is to "retire rich," like so many books promise to help you do, but that's not the end goal. My goal in teaching financial principles to my children is not so they will become rich; it's so they can have a better life with true wealth in more than just a monetary sense. I don't want them to grow up to love money. Not only does the Bible warn against the love of money (1 Timothy 6:10), but I've never met a happy person who loves money.

### 4. Time is More Valuable Than Money

The CEOs of the largest companies in the world are not without money, but do they have happiness? Strong marriages? Time for themselves and family? Often, when you rise to the top, the sacrifice of your time and personal life is so great that all you have to show for it is money.

Simply put, between time and money, the one you can't earn more of is more important than the one you can. Sadly, it seems to take around 10 years of our adult life, on average, to learn this. We work hard, rarely see our families, and then wake up one day and realize the world has been going on around us for the last 10 years while we were re-living Groundhog Day at work, always trying to earn more money, always trying to get that next promotion.

Teach your children to have a healthy focus on living, and spending time with the people they love, rather than only on money.

### 5. It's Always Better to Be Debt Free

I won't beat the debt topic to death… because we'll discuss debt later in this book, but I think we all agree: revolving credit card balances are bad, payday loans are a scam, and we shouldn't have car payments if we can help it. I want to focus more on what's known as "good debt" to so many people.

Relax, debt-lovers. I'm not saying this "good debt" stuff is all bad, but I want to make sure your kids are educated on what it really means. Teaching your kids about debt will depend a lot on how you view debt, so let's make sure we're forming our own healthy viewpoints. Your children need guidance, and the less they owe, the better off they will be. Many people use debt as leverage to buy things like real estate at a much faster rate. The problem is, it can be a risky business.

Think about the success-turned-failure stories you hear about former millionaires who lost everything. It's because of debt almost every time. We'll stick with the real estate example. It's true, if you want to invest in real estate, you can use leverage to buy more houses, at a faster rate. You can buy an investment property, and then use the equity to take out another loan, and you can continue this process as long as you keep enough equity in your homes, and as long as the bank will keep lending you money.

The problem here is, you have to hope nothing drastically changes. All it takes is one huge downshift in the economy, or your specific housing market, to totally take out your portfolio. It happens all the time. It's happening as I write this book. The 2020 coronavirus outbreak has caused people all over the country to lose their jobs, which means they can't pay rent. What happens to the landlords who are counting on that rent to pay their mortgages? If they're heavily leveraged (read: buried in debt), without enough liquid money (read: actual cash) in the bank, they're going to lose those properties.

The Bible says the borrower is slave to the lender (Proverbs 22:7), and these types of scenarios show exactly how true that is. That doesn't mean it's a sin to be in debt, but that proverb is one of God's warnings against it.

An even bigger concern than the slave thing (which is a big concern), is the greed factor. You know, greed—one of the most mentioned sins in the Bible, yet one of the least discussed in church. When you start to see how much you can get with debt, it's easy to get greedy.

Think about two real-estate scenarios, since real estate and business ownership are the two main areas in which people get into extreme amounts of debt. I'm going to keep these scenarios extremely simple to show my point. I won't cover maintenance costs, taxes, unexpected events, etc. I'll keep the numbers simple and rounded, but if you just absolutely hate math, feel free to skip this section.

**Note:** Don't get caught up on the amounts, because it varies from state to state. You can find a small rental home for $75,000 in the Midwest, while $400,000 will barely get you a fixer-upper on the West Coast. Remember that the point of this section is to explain a concept, not to give current, realistic-to-everyone numbers.

*Scenario 1: Leverage*

Let's say you buy an investment property on a $200,000 mortgage, with a $2,000/month payment, and you receive $2,200/month in rent for this home. While you have the loan, you have a surplus of $200/month. Once you have 20% equity in your home (meaning you still owe $160,000), you use that equity to take out another $200,000 loan, which you receive another $200/month surplus from ($2,200/month rent).

You now have $400/month in surplus, rental income each month, and you're in $360,000 of debt. You don't own $400,000 worth of real estate, you only truly own what you have in equity, so you own the $40,000, but you're responsible for $400,000 of property. Your total rental income is $400 at the moment.

Now let's look at another option...

*Scenario 2: Single Mortgages*

In this scenario, you still buy the first home. You pay the same amount and receive the same surplus. But instead of taking out a second mortgage, you work really hard and pay the first home off entirely. The entire time, you've had the extra $200/month to put towards the mortgage, and you've been paying much more on top of that to get this thing paid off.

Once it's paid off, you now have $2,200 in monthly rental income and $0 in debt. So now you buy another home on a $200,000 mortgage. With your second home, you receive the same $200 surplus to put towards paying this home off, except now you have an additional $2,200 on top of that (from your first home) to pay down your second mortgage.

Even if you put $0 down on your second home (which isn't likely to be an option anyway), you now own $200,000 (equity) of real estate, and you receive $2,400/month in rental cash flow (profit). If anything were to happen, you have a huge amount of equity in your portfolio to work with, and a much higher net worth than in the first scenario.

This scenario is like compound interest: in the beginning it's a slow-go, but as it builds up, you can buy more real estate faster and faster. In 20 or 30 years, with scenario 1, you could be sitting with six or seven homes for a total of $100,000 in equity (aka net worth), or you could own four homes, with a mortgage on one, for a total equity of over $600,000.

Sure, the math will never really be this simple, but I hope it at least makes you think about proposing options like this to your children.

*One More Scenario*

The third scenario would be similar to the second, but saving and paying cash for the first house so you're never in debt. This is possible, and your kids could do this and be debt-free forever.

It's not common to do things debt-free, but it's always going to be the least stressful, and most beneficial plan over time. I'm not talking about who can make the most money; I'm talking about a plan where your financial well-being isn't dependent upon a bank.

None of these options were meant to be the best for everyone, but it is important to know that your kids *have* options.

## 6. Outsource What You Can

If you're not good at something, or prefer to focus on your specific talent, outsource the other stuff. Delegation. This applies to business owners and individuals. There are plenty of inexpensive services that allow you to outsource the tedious tasks of business and life. It's necessary to have a network in place that allows you to function at the highest level. That network is created through outsourcing.

Why outsource? Refer back to point #4. Outsourcing is a way to get your time back. Do a quick calculation and determine if outsourcing frees up enough time for you to do something more valuable with that time.

A simple, real-life example is lawn care. If you love to mow your grass, then do it. Some people find it soothing and relaxing. If you don't like it, and you can find something more valuable to do with that time, outsource it. Now take this concept to other areas of your life.

This is a good idea to instill into your children. Our time is finite, so if we want to do big things with our lives, we have to come up with ways to "create" more time and margin in our lives. Getting into the mindset of outsourcing is a great first step towards getting that margin in life. While children won't be outsourcing their chores or their homework, they can still understand the concept for immediate implementation upon moving out. Simple conversations about it is all you need.

**7. Insure What You Can't Afford to Replace**

In 2011, a good friend of mine lost several rental properties in a bad storm. He did the debt-free thing so well, he owned all of them in full. The problem was, when you actually own your home, you don't technically have to keep insurance on it anymore. He chose not to. It turned out to be a mistake. He couldn't afford to replace the homes, so he lost thousands in monthly income, overnight. The ironic part is, he's the one who taught me the concept of "insure what you can't afford to replace." We tend to take on the that-could-never-happen-to-me mindset. That's a dangerous mindset.

Make sure your children are savvy on all types of insurance. Insurance is something we all hate to pay for, but we all need in one way or another at some point in life. If you pass down the "insure what you can't afford to replace" mindset to your kids, they won't run into major setbacks without having a way out.

Summary – Money Lessons

**9 Things to Know Before Leaving Home**

1. How to open and manage accounts
2. The importance of giving
3. How to be a savvy shopper
4. How debt can ruin your life
5. Why credit isn't that important
6. How budgets give you freedom
7. The power of automation
8. How to nail a job interview
9. How insurance works

**9 Concepts to Know**

1. Compound interest
2. Diversification
3. Dollar-cost averaging
4. Inflation
5. Mutual fund
6. Net worth

7. Opportunity cost
8. Rule of 72
9. Tax

**7 Pieces of Money Wisdom**

1. Mindset is the key.
2. Buy assets, not liabilities.
3. Measure by net worth.
4. Time is more valuable than money.
5. It's always better to be debt free.
6. Outsource what you can.
7. Insure what you can't afford to replace.

FOUR

# WORK ETHIC

A SYSTEM TO PAY AND TEACH YOUR KIDS

"It is not what you do for your children, but what you have taught them to do for themselves that will make them successful human beings."

ANN LANDERS, ADVICE COLUMNIST FOR *ASK ANN LANDERS*

"Don't be afraid to give your best to what seemingly are small jobs. Every time you conquer one it makes you that much stronger. If you do little jobs well, the big ones will tend to take care of themselves."

DALE CARNEGIE, AUTHOR OF *HOW TO WIN FRIENDS AND INFLUENCE PEOPLE*

"The dictionary is the only place where success comes before work. Work is the key to success, and hard work can help you accomplish anything."

VINCE LOMBARDI, FORMER HEAD COACH OF THE GREEN BAY PACKERS

---

IN HIS FAMOUS BOOK, *RICH DAD POOR DAD: WHAT THE RICH Teach Their Kids About Money That the Poor and Middle Class Do Not!*, Robert Kiyosaki recalls a story from when he was a kid. His "rich dad" told him he would have to "make money" if he wanted to be rich. Naturally, he went around the neighborhood with his friend, collecting Crest toothpaste tubes. The Crest tubes were made out of lead back then. The two kids proceeded to melt down the lead and pour it into molds they had created out of plaster of paris by using real coins. They were making counterfeit money and they didn't even know what counterfeit meant.

What's the moral of this story? We can't leave it up to our kids to figure out how to make money and where it comes from. Children will initially think money comes from mom and dad, because initially it does. That's all they know. It's our job to teach children where money comes from in the real world. You can begin teaching this with their allowance (or whatever you decide to call it). You'll have to come up with your own system of how you pay your children, and what they get paid for. We've tried plenty of methods with our kids, and I'll share what works for us.

Beth Kobliner, author of *Make Your Kid a Money Genius (Even If You're Not): A Parents' Guide for Kids 3 to 23*, says an allowance is important, but you shouldn't link an allowance with chores.[1] She also says you shouldn't "bribe" kids by paying them for good grades or behavior.[2] Dave Ramsey, co-author of *Smart Money Smart Kids: Raising the Next Generation to Win With Money*, says an allowance is useless and you should put your kids on commission (only paying kids if they complete chores).[3] They're both great teachers, with great ideas and great books.

No matter which theory you lean towards, the basic idea is the same: don't pay your kids for no reason. Whatever your opinion is on the matter, let me share with you the system we use with our five children, for your consideration.

Rent Vs. PayCheck

Just as some people prefer the terms "allowance" or "commission," we use our own terms: "rent" and "paycheck." Those are the two categories our kids' pay falls into. Also, we use the term "chore" synonymously with "job," as in a one-time job. We want our kids to understand it's not free to live in a home.

Here's how it works:

- **Rent** – Each child has a certain chore, depending on their age, which pays their share of the rent. If they don't complete this, they have to pay rent. If they do complete this, they've paid their rent. If they have to pay rent, we just charge a dollar for each undone chore that would pay their rent if completed. It doesn't have to be a high amount. If they know they

have to pay for not completing a task, that's typically enough motivation.
- **Paycheck** – Likewise, each child has a chore they're paid for. This is their weekly paycheck.

We make these payments on the same day each week to teach the concept of a real paycheck. When everyone is completing all their chores, everything goes well, and our home functions like any other home that pays their children for work. It's when our kids start slacking that things get interesting.

If someone doesn't complete their paycheck chore(s), they don't get paid for that day. The older kids have multiple chores with an amount for each, so it's possible to get paid for one and not another. If someone fails to complete all of their paycheck chores for three days in a row, they can be fired. I say "can be" because obviously different life events play a role here. If they're fired, the other kids have the opportunity to apply for the job. We have a job interview (teaching interview skills as we go), and someone else takes on the responsibility (typically for one week and then the job goes back to the original owner, depending on how many times this has happened).

What's interesting is *who* pays the new-hire. The child who got fired pays the child who took over their job. This is a week of reflection for that child, and they're more than happy to take their job back, and stop paying their sibling, after that week. It helps them tie *losing their job* to *financial hardship,* on their level.

FirstKidBank.com (Beta version, as of 2020) is a free tool you can use to keep track of your children's weekly paychecks. We just use a spreadsheet on the wall by the door. That way they see it every day, remember to do their work, and we can easily mark off the work that has been done. Either tool works.

## Running the "Family Business"

This may sound like a complicated system at first, but it's easy to implement. There is a period of adjustment, but it's a fair system that doesn't foster unhealthy competitive spirits in our home.

Our kids don't fight for each other's jobs or anything crazy like that. Maybe they would if we hadn't explained why we do this system. Now they understand the basics of having a job, doing well to keep their job, and what it feels like to get fired. Some parents love our system. Others have criticized us for being strict or for making our kids' lives stressful. I think it would stress out our kids if we ran this business like dictators, but we do it out of love and with an educational purpose.

Seriously, our kids couldn't be happier with this system. They have the opportunity to make quite a bit of money—even more than their weekly paycheck, as I'll show you soon.

Our kids have learned more about work and life from this method than any other method we've ever implemented. It's all in how you administer it, and how you make use of the important conversations this method creates. That's where the real value comes from: the crucial conversations.

## Odd Jobs and Negotiation Skills

Negotiation skills are becoming a lost art, but negotiation can be taught at home. The best way to do this, and for our kids to earn extra cash, is through odd jobs.

When one of our kids wants to make some extra money, they can look around the house to find extra work. If they see something that needs to be done, they come to us with a proposal:

what needs to be done and how much they're willing to do it for. We can either accept their offer, decline their offer (explaining why), or negotiate. We prefer to negotiate, for their sake.

Here's a recent scenario:

> **Child:** "I noticed there are a lot of rocks, from the gravel part of our yard, that have made their way into the grassy part of our yard. I am willing to pick up all those rocks for $10."
>
> **Us:** "Let's go check it out."
>
> *We see there are plenty of rocks scattered throughout the grass, which creates a problem for the mower and weed eater, so we decide the job needs to be done.*
>
> **Us:** "We would like you to pick up the rocks, but $10 is high for a job that looks like it will take less than one hour. How about $5?"
>
> *In the beginning, they would usually take whatever we offered, but we've taught them to at least try to negotiate.*
>
> **Child:** "$10 may be too high, but the work is tedious and I'm saving you guys from having to do it. What about $7?"
>
> **Us:** "$7 it is, but only if you do a good job, and get the vast majority of the rocks. If we have to come behind you and pick up several additional rocks, we will still pay you $5. Does that work for you?"
>
> **Child:** "Yup! I'm on it."

In this scenario, knowing they will make less money if they

don't do a good job, they will typically get every rock. They learn the value of negotiation, and the value of "getting paid what you're worth." The harder they work, the more they earn.

## It Takes Work

This system requires parental dedication. The main thing is staying on top of your kids and keeping up with their pay. It's not something you can tell your kids you're doing, and then forget about it. They will take this extremely seriously if you do, and it requires you to check (and check off) their work every day. If you tell them they can be fired after so many days of not completing their paycheck chores, then you must follow through.

Again, make sure you pay them consistently. Find a good day of the week (typically on the weekend) and hand out their paycheck(s). Don't forget to get the single bills before payday. There will be times when you forget and you have to postpone their paycheck for a day or two but keep this as rare as possible. Or, use a digital system like the website mentioned earlier. Either way, *show them* when they get paid.

Another option is to print off pretend checks, and actually give them a physical paycheck. This is great for kids to understand checks, and the concept of receiving a paycheck. Plus, for younger kids, it may be better than having them personally keep track of dollar bills. Don't forget to keep track of how much you're allocating to them, so you're not blindsided when they want to get their money later.

If you take this system seriously, so will your kids. It's a great outline for you to create your own similar scenario or use this exact system. Find what works for you, implement it, and stick with it.

All this talk of hard work leads us into a topic that can't go without mentioning: grit.

## How to Instill Grit and Work Ethic

Grit is a learned character trait. It separates the ordinary from the extraordinary. So, what exactly is grit? The word "grit" may trigger thoughts of hardened cowboys, but grit is getting a new identity. It's being used in the psychological sense more and more. And that's what we're talking about here: mental grit.

Merriam-Webster defines grit as "firmness of mind or spirit: unyielding courage in the face of hardship or danger." In psychology, grit is defined as, "a positive, non-cognitive trait based on an individual's perseverance of effort combined with the passion for a particular long-term goal or end state (a powerful motivation to achieve an objective)."

Practically anything you read about grit is going to open with Angela Duckworth's research. She's the author of a book called, *Grit: The Power of Passion and Perseverance*, and she's been studying the idea for years. Cindra Kamphoff wrote somewhat of a sequel to that book: *Beyond Grit: Ten Powerful Practices to Gain the High-Performance Edge*. I've read and highly recommend both.

Other than compassion and a charitable heart, grit may be the next most important character trait your children can learn. The successful people of the world rarely did it on intelligence alone, and many of the *most successful* people admit they aren't the smartest, but they're all the grittiest in one way or another.

So how is grit taught? You can start with a few practices. This is a process.

**1. Reframe Failure**

Your home is a safe place in which your child can fail. You should be a safe person for your child to fail in front of. Mistakes and failures are some of the greatest teachers, *if we frame them that way*. It's the simple act of instilling in your children that failure is a positive thing when we learn from it. As John Maxwell would say, "fail forward."

Let your children fail. Don't step in and rescue your kids before they have a chance to experience failure. You will be missing the opportunity to coach them in understanding a possible lesson to learn from the failure.

**2. Allow Challenge**

Don't be the parent who takes all opportunities for challenge away from your children. It's tough to see your kids struggling with something. You want to help them, but you've got to let them do it on their own.

I've heard people who came from broken childhoods say they feel sorry for kids who are raised in a good home, because they never got the opportunity to deal with true adversity. That's why some of the most successful and happiest people came from the worst childhoods.

I'm not saying you should give your kid a bad childhood, but allowing controlled challenges is the closest, and safest, way to instill grit in your kids. In fact, when your child grows up in a good home, that's the *only way* for them to get experience with adversity. And that's important experience!

**3. Encourage Constantly**

Encouragement has to come along with learning from failure and handling challenges. The goal here is to build your children up, not tear them down. Sure, failure and challenges will tear them down a little bit, but you'll build them up ten times more.

Our words are important. Think of all the things people said to you when you were a kid. Things they may not remember, but you do. We can't take our words back once they leave our mouths, so make them count, and speak positivity into your children's lives.

Here's a recap of the 3-part process:

1. Reframe failure
2. Allow challenge
3. Encourage constantly

If you follow this pattern, your children will see failure in a positive light. They will accept the challenge, fail occasionally, learn from the failure, overcome obstacles, and fully accept your encouragement along the way.

When it comes to success—whatever that ends up meaning for your children—grit seems to be the common denominator that makes it happen. The ability to focus on and achieve a goal is not common. Grit is what separates those who *do* from those who merely *talk*. Grit is a mental toughness. A *real* toughness.

## Summary – Work Ethic

### Where Money Comes From
Children need to understand money isn't free; it is earned. The basic rule of thumb is, pay your children for a reason. Tie working into earning, and tie earning into having money.

### Rent Vs. Paycheck
Our children pay their "rent" with their chores. They receive a "paycheck" for their additional duties.

If they don't put in the work, they don't get the paycheck. Likewise, if they don't do the chores that pay the rent, they have to pay rent.

### Running the "Family Business"
Consider implementing a system to run your children's pay like a business. If the work doesn't get done three days in a row, the child can be fired. Whoever takes over the job is paid by the one who got fired. This ties job loss into financial hardship, on their level.

Teach your kids to negotiate with odd jobs around the house.

### How to Instill Grit and Work Ethic
Grit is defined as "firmness of mind or spirit: unyielding courage in the face of hardship or danger." In psychology, grit is defined as, "a positive, non-cognitive trait based on an individual's perseverance of effort combined with the passion for a

particular long-term goal or end state (a powerful motivation to achieve an objective)."

To instill grit in our children, we must:

1. Reframe failure
2. Allow challenge
3. Encourage constantly

# FIVE
# MONEY MANAGEMENT
## BUDGETING AT EVERY AGE

"Budgets are not merely affairs of arithmetic, but in a thousand ways go to the root of the prosperity of individuals, the relation of classes, and the strength of kingdoms."

WILLIAM E. GLADSTONE, BRITISH STATESMAN AND POLITICIAN

"If we command our wealth, we shall be rich and free. If our wealth commands us, we are poor indeed."

EDMUND BURKE, ANGLO-IRISH STATESMAN AND PHILOSOPHER

---

OUR HOME BUDGET BEGAN WITH THE ENVELOPE SYSTEM. WE USED A separate envelope for each category. Once the envelope ran out of money, we couldn't spend any more in that category until the following month. That's the system we used to budget while we were getting out of debt, and it worked wonders. Now we use an app that calculates the entire thing for us. Technology has evolved. But there's no one-size-fits-all budget. Everyone has a personal preference. You can help your kids find theirs.

Budgeting is a simple concept that can be difficult in practice. We all know the basics of what a budget is, but most people don't follow one. Seriously, most people, regardless of what they say, don't follow a budget, according to a recent Gallup poll.[1] Around 32% of Americans follow a budget regularly.

That's around the same percentage as Americans with a long-term plan for their finances.[2]

Coincidence?

Before we can teach budgeting to our kids, we've got to understand the basics ourselves, and for our kids to actually listen to us, we had better be following one.

## Budgeting Basics

Starting a budget as an adult is simple. I can break it down into five steps:

1. Track your expenses and income for one month.
2. Create the categories that fit your life.
3. Set some short-term and long-term financial goals.
4. Reduce some spending areas to make those goals possible.
5. Adjust your budget accordingly over time.

The most important step here is the last step, because that's what builds the budgeting habit. The most common budget killer I've seen is unexpected expenses.

I'll watch someone track their expenses, set a budget, and stick with it… all the way up to some event causing them to spend an unexpected amount of money. That blows one of the categories, and causes the budget to unravel for that month, and then they give up.

A budget is a living thing. It's constantly changing with your life, and you shouldn't expect it to stay the same, because life doesn't stay the same. These are all things kids will need to know before they go out and try to create their own budget, but first, we need to meet kids where they're at. So let's talk about budgeting at each age…

**Budgeting (Ages 3-5)**

At this age, kids can start learning the importance of giving, but they also need the freedom to spend most of their money so they can start learning what that feels like. Three years old is about the youngest age we've implemented the give/save/spend jars, but the emphasis is on the give and spend jars.

If you have a super gracious child who wants to give most of their money and spend very little, it's best to encourage more of a balance. A 10% savings goal is reasonable at this age, but for giving and spending, anywhere from 10%/80% to 45%/45% works.

Children need visually stimulating incentives at this age. Get a large, clear jar, and use actual dollar bills to fill it up for savings. Let them physically give their own money at church, or wherever you decide to give. And give them their own money to spend when they're making a purchase, but you may be the one to hold on to the money until they're ready to spend it.

**Budgeting (Ages 6-11)**

By this age, you'll be able to tell if your child is more of a "saver" or a "spender." You can start to encourage them to do a little more of whichever one feels *less* natural. If you don't, it could turn into a bad spending habit or a money-hoarding problem later on.

Once your kid reaches that sixth birthday, it's time to put more emphasis on saving, and get specific with the percentage your child wants to save. Are they saving 20%? 30%? Whatever percentage you go with, set it in stone by this age. They're old enough to understand how to save for something, and purchase it, but it's likely they don't quite have the discipline to save large amounts of money.

It's time to let them save for something big (preferably a few hundred dollars) and then let them buy it. If they want to adjust their jar percentages at this time, feel free to let them, but again, if you reset the percentages, make the new ones firm.

**Budgeting (Ages 12-14)**

It's time for the car talk. Before now, decide whether they're buying their own car, you're buying the car, or a mixture of the two. Once they hit the tween stage, they need to know the plan so they can do their part. We'll go into great depth about buying your kid's first car in the next chapter.

If you've allowed them to spend their own money for the last few years, they should already be accustomed to the value of money, and how giving, saving, and spending work. If that's the case, budgeting will be natural from here.

**Budgeting (Ages 15-18)**

At this age, your children should start seeing some of their own expenses. Things like a cellphone or car insurance. Now it's time for the debt talk, since a vehicle is typically the first debt trap. You can help your kids stay debt-free forever if they want to be.

It's time to start showing them the family finances in full detail. Let them see what a budget looks like. Have your teen set categories for their own budget. It should be a simple version of a family budget, and it would just include things like entertainment, eating out, car insurance, cellphone, etc. If you're a Dave Ramsey fan, you can introduce them to Dave's Baby Steps at this point.[3]

Introduce the concept of investing by adding a "grow" jar to the other three jars. At this point, they likely won't still be using physical jars, but the concept remains the same. By now, they should have their own checking and savings accounts.

Before they leave home, create a sample budget with them, especially if they're moving out immediately upon graduating high school to attend college. Your children can avoid money problems if they grow up learning all of these concepts gradually, over time.

## Emergency Funds

According to Murphy's Law, random expenses will seem to

flood your life, until you're prepared with an emergency fund, then the unexpected will subside.

Forty percent of Americans don't have the savings to cover a $400 unexpected expense, according to the Federal Reserve.[4] This explains why credit card debt is getting higher and higher. The last thing you want your kids to do in an emergency is turn to credit cards. The second to last thing you want is for them to turn to the National Bank of Mom & Dad. An emergency fund reduces the chances of both.

When your children are just moving out, it's a good idea for them to have saved at least $500 for emergencies in a savings account. Six months of living expenses is the ultimate goal for the fund. Think of this as "bare bones" living for six months. This is easy to calculate. Just imagine how you would spend money if you lost your job (i.e., no eating out, no extra entertainment, etc.), and come up with how much you would need to pay all of your bills for a month. Then multiply that by six. If you want to give your children a monetary gift when they leave home, consider giving them the gift of financial security: an emergency fund. But don't feel obligated.

Summary – Money Management

**Budgeting at Every Age**
Budgeting is easy when learned young. Teach your kids how budgets are a good thing, and not a "necessary evil."

You can teach more budgeting concepts as kids get older, but start when they're young, and teach them age-appropriate skills.

**Budgeting Basics**

To start budgeting:

1. Track your expenses and income for one month.
2. Create the categories that fit your life.
3. Set some short-term and long-term financial goals.
4. Reduce some spending areas to make those goals possible.
5. Adjust your budget accordingly over time.

**Emergency Funds**

Help your kids to leave home with at least $500 in an emergency fund, with a goal of saving a fully-funded emergency fund (six months of living expenses).

## SIX
# TRANSPORTATION
### BUYING THAT FIRST CAR

"The car has become an article of dress without which we feel uncertain, unclad, and incomplete in the urban compound."

MARSHALL MCLUHAN, A CORNERSTONE PHILOSOPHER IN THE STUDY OF MEDIA THEORY

"Americanism: Using money you haven't earned to buy things you don't need to impress people you don't like."

ROBERT QUILLEN, SYNDICATED HUMORIST, FROM A JUNE 1928 COLUMN

---

My friend, Greg, bought a new car last year. His car had broken down three times in the few weeks prior to buying his new car, and each time it left him stranded on the side of the road. He was sick of dealing with it, and he didn't want another vehicle with the same problems. He was fed up, so after the third breakdown, he scrapped his car, and went straight to the dealership.

Greg used the $200 he got for scrapping his car to pay basically nothing down on a $55,000 BMW. Yes, he went to a BMW dealership of all places. He didn't get pre-approved or look for a lower interest rate (his credit isn't great), so he's paying over $1,000/month for his new car... for the next five years. He's car-poor now: he can't afford to do much of anything outside of working to pay off his car... and this was supposedly a solution to reduce stress. In one moment—or one emotion—Greg went from not having a car payment to having an eleven-hundred-dollar car payment, every month, for years to come. He solved a temporary problem with a permanent solution. This is the situation many Americans find themselves in today. It all stems from having an improper view of vehicle ownership. If you give your kids a responsible view of vehicle ownership, they'll already be so far ahead of the majority, because the majority are car-poor, which we'll talk about more in the next few pages.

The average car payment is over $500/month, according to an Experian report from 2018.[1] Another report, from the U.S. Public Interest Research Group (PIRG), shows auto debt has risen 75% since the Great Recession of 2009.[2]

The PIRG study showed some interesting insight into why auto debt and car payments have gotten so high:

*"Auto lending rebounded from the Great Recession in part because of low interest rates (fueled by the Federal Reserve Board's policy of quantitative easing) and a perception by lenders that auto loans had held up better than mortgages during the financial crisis. As one*

*hedge fund manager noted in a 2017 interview with The Financial Times, during the recession, '[c]onsumers tended to default on their house first, credit card second, and car third.'"*

The study goes on to explain the ways auto lenders have preyed on consumers...

### Auto-Lender Predators

Auto lenders have their tactics. They're in a trillion-dollar industry, and their goal is to do whatever it takes to make you finance more than you need, and often more than you can afford. Here are some of the tactics used by auto lenders:

- **Confusing Terms** – Providing incomplete or confusing information about the terms of the loan, including interest rates.
- **Inappropriate Loans** – Making loans to people without the ability to repay.
- **Discrimination** – Discriminatory markups of loans that result in African-American and Hispanic borrowers paying more for auto loans.
- **Unnecessary Additions** – Pushing expensive "add-ons" such as insurance products, extended warranties and overpriced vehicle options, the cost of which is added to a consumer's loan.
- **Abusive Tactics** – Engaging in abusive collection and repossession tactics once a consumer's loan has become past due.

There are plenty of "discount" auto sales companies we

drive by every day. You know them, the ones with the "bad credit welcome" and "no interest for 90 days" signs. The places where used car salesmen get their reputation for being sleazy. We've all witnessed the bullying tactics used by many car dealers, to include the, "let me bring my manager in," tactic when you seem hesitant. And even the old, "I'm going to guilt you into buying a car you already told me you didn't want," tactic.

*The New York Times* published an article about Yvette Harris, a citizen of New York, who bought a used 1997 Mitsubishi for an outrageous price and was still stuck with the payments in 2017 —over 10 years after the vehicle was repossessed.[3]

Nagham Jawad, a refugee from Iraq, bought a Chevy Tahoe in 2009. The transmission went out a few months later. It was so expensive to fix, the lender didn't even bother repossessing it, but Nagham was still liable for the loan for the next few years.

These stories aren't unique. The vast majority of Americans are uneducated when it comes to auto loans, interest rates, and ultimately… debt in general. Our job is to make sure our children understand how dangerous these types of loans can be, and why it's best to avoid them altogether.

### Car-Poor Americans

Car payments. They keep people from having a solid retirement fund. They keep Americans poor. It's not lattes and impulse buys; more often, it's car payments.

Five hundred dollars every month, invested at an 8% interest rate, over an entire typical adult lifetime, would be over $2 million, but people would rather have a new car than money. They may not admit to that; they may not even realize it's true. I get it, you want a nice car, but there are ways to save and wait until you can actually afford a nice car. If you have to finance it, you can't afford it. If you decide to finance it anyway, at least get a vehicle that won't keep you poor forever.

A good rule of thumb is to pay no more than 5x your monthly salary for a vehicle. Figure out that amount, save first, and then buy it once you have the money. Teach your children to make car payments to themselves in an interest-bearing account (e.g., municipal bonds, high-interest money market account, etc.), instead of making car payments to a company... and paying interest.

**Why are People Living the Car-Poor Life?**

*Car-Poor* is the mindset of always planning to have a car payment.

Why do people do that? It comes down to three Ps:

1. **Past** – They have always had car payments, and think car payments are [and will always be] part of life.
2. **Pride** – They don't want to be seen in an older, not-as-nice vehicle so they spend their entire life paying for a car to impress other people who don't care what they drive in the first place.
3. **Priorities** – They want a nicer vehicle than they can afford and they've decided buying this vehicle is more important than having this amount of money for retirement or anything else.

When I first did the math on how much vehicles would cost me over my lifetime, I simply couldn't bring myself to buy a new or really nice car. I just couldn't let myself pay over $50,000 for a vehicle I'm going to use less than an hour a day, on average.

Vehicles are expensive and they are constantly in situations to be damaged (e.g., parking lots, storms, bad drivers, driving in general). When choosing a vehicle, carefully compare all of the options available.

## Reframing Our View of Vehicles

Buying a new car is great… for a few months. Until the new-car smell fades and you get complacent. It happens to everyone. You love your new car for a while, and then it's just like your last car. Were those few months worth the extra $50k?

If you typically buy new cars and you're used to having a large car payment, just ask yourself this question: "why do I choose to buy a newer vehicle, over an older, reliable one?" And don't use the "newer vehicles are safer and I don't have to worry as much about maintenance" answer. First, that's not always true (especially the safety part), and second, is that really worth $500k over your lifetime? Stop and think.

All I am asking is that you redirect your thinking. If you drive an expensive car, ask yourself why. Could you be satisfied with a less expensive car if it performed really well? If we have a healthy view of vehicles, our kids can much more easily adopt a healthy view of vehicles.

## Paying for the Car

As a parent, is it your responsibility to pay for your kid's car? As a responsible adult-in-training, is it their responsibility to pay for their own car? Or should you give them a little boost, but not all of the money? Or perhaps you could match what they save?

The short answer is "yes." There's no right or wrong here, but I can give you some ideas and options. Here are four:

1. **You pay for the car.** Some parents want to provide a car for their child. There's nothing wrong with that, but I do believe people take better care of things when they are personally invested. Of course, it's your prerogative.
2. **They pay for the car.** Saving your own money and paying your own way can teach work ethic. It can teach the value of delayed gratification (the opposite of impulse buying). It can teach discipline. If your kids pay their own way, they will learn how life works, early on.
3. **You get them started.** A little boost would be nice. Maybe $500 or $1,000 towards the car. That would be helpful. You wouldn't be leaving them to fend for themselves, but you wouldn't be fully providing their ride either.
4. **You match what they save.** If your child saves $1,000, they can buy a $2,000 car. If they save $15,000, they can buy a $30,000 car. If you choose this route, I suggest saving the money in a separate account, at the same rate as your child. For parents with several children, this may not always be the most feasible option, but I think it's the best of both worlds.

My wife and I are taking option #4. With five children, we know it will cost us a lot, but there are a few reasons we chose this route. We believe it, 1) encourages them to save, 2) allows us to bless them, and 3) simultaneously puts some of their own skin in the game. We know our children will save at different rates. We monitor closely to make sure we're saving the same amount so we're not blindsided by a $10,000 match down the road.

**Who Should Pay for the Car Insurance?**

Younger kids will be much more expensive to insure than older kids. Paying for insurance is like paying for the car: you have options. You can pay all, part, or none of their insurance and those are all fine options.

Your primary duty is to help them *find* a reasonable car that's safe and affordable, including being affordable over the life of the car. You must consider insurance and maintenance in the cost. There are some discounts, like the "Good Student Discount," they can apply for. For this discount, your child must:

- Be under 25 years old.
- Maintain a 3.0 GPA or higher.
- Show status of being a good student.
- Be enrolled in high school or college full time.

We will pay for part of our children's insurance. If they want a car with a higher premium, they'll have to pay the difference. You have to find what works for you.

**Who Pays for Gas and Maintenance?**

Encourage your children to have an emergency fund for their car. It's likely the only thing they have to worry about maintaining, so this shouldn't be too difficult. Five hundred dollars is typically a good amount to cover most unexpected expenses and routine maintenance, but it never hurts to save more.

The more we, as parents, pay for some things here and there, the more we show involvement. Whichever way you go, let it be intentional, and well laid out for your children.

Our children will pay their own maintenance, but we will pay for gas. You could reverse that, or again, you could go with the "pay all" or "pay none" method.

**Should Your Children Get a Car Loan?**

No. Next question.

Ok, ok. Is it obvious that I hate debt? I think it's dangerous to put your child [or allow them to go] into debt. An 18-year-old honestly doesn't need a car expensive enough to require a loan. If they want to go down that road (no pun intended) later in life, leave it up to them. If you do decide to take out a loan for some reason, please, please, please read the next section...

**Should You Co-Sign for Your Children?**

When someone (i.e., your child) needs a co-signer, that means the lender doesn't think they're going to pay up. That should tell you something. Not only that, but this could damage your relationship with your child if they do stop making payments. Don't justify the decision by saying you are "helping them build credit," or something along those lines. If your children don't pay, you're just showing them mom and dad will bail them out.

If you do decide to co-sign, after the above warning, here are some things to consider:

1. Make sure you agree with the purchase.
2. Make sure you can afford to pay the loan.
3. Make sure you will be notified if they don't pay.
4. Make sure you understand all the consequences.
5. Make sure you read your state's laws on co-signing.

Again, I recommend not co-signing at all. Here's what you could do instead:

1. Explain why it's a bad idea to co-sign.
2. Suggest they not take the loan at all.
3. Help them learn to save for big purchases.
4. Explain that your relationship is more important.
5. Explain why they shouldn't co-sign for other people, either.

If you've already co-signed, hopefully your child will pay the loan and everything will be fine. Here are some steps to take if the co-sign has already gone south:

1. **Attempt to work out a payment plan with your child.** If you are still in contact with them, they may be willing to at least help pay the loan, since they can't pay it in full.
2. **Call the lender and negotiate the agreement.** The lender may be willing to work with you, especially if

you aren't able to pay. They would rather get something than nothing. You may be able to negotiate a lower interest rate and/or a lower balance, but don't let them bully you or talk down to you.
3. **Stay disciplined and learn from this.** It may have been a bad idea for you to co-sign, but you can't change the past, so why not learn from it? I doubt you will ever do it again. The good news is, this can be the last time you ever do it. Hard-won lessons typically stick.

## Finding a Great Deal on Your Kid's Car

Odds are, you'll want your children to have a nice enough car so you know it will get them from A to B, but not a brand new car with a factory warranty. Fortunately, there are plenty of ways to find a good deal on a nice, reliable, used car.

First, you have to know what you're looking for. Once you've determined how the funding is going to work, you should have an idea of how much you can spend. Cars.com is a good place to find the type of car your child would prefer. You can also get the Consumer Report annual reviews for the different makes/models your child likes.[4] It's better to have an idea of what you're looking for, rather than a specific car in mind. The more flexible you are, the better your chances of finding a great deal.

You have two basic options when buying a car:

1. **Buy from a Dealer** – Many people choose this option, because it seems safer (until the dealers surround you like a pack of wild dogs). Honestly, there are benefits

to dealerships. You have multiple options right in front of you. You can test drive all kinds of different vehicles. But you'll pay for that convenience. Buying from a dealership is much more expensive than buying from a private party. Just look at the cost comparison on Kelly Blue Book,[5] and see how high dealer prices are, compared to private parties.
2. **Buy from a Private Seller** – This is the more affordable option. Your money will go farther. But it is a little more of a hassle. You'll have to meet with multiple people to see multiple cars. Granted, that's a small price to pay for saving thousands of dollars.

Once you've decided *how* to buy, here are some tips to get the best deal for your kid's first car:

- **Don't let your kid get married to the car.** They may fall in love with it immediately, but letting those emotions get involved will cost them. The seller—especially car dealers—want you to fall in love with the purchase. It makes their job easier.
- **Don't be afraid to walk away.** The ability to walk away from a potential purchase holds a tremendous amount of power. The seller wants to make money and they need a buyer to do that. If they aren't willing to negotiate, run!
- **Be informed from the start.** When you see the type of car your child wants to look at, help them get all the information about the car: the value, the specs, the features, etc. If possible, get a CARFAX Report ahead of time. [6] These reports will only show what has

actually been reported, so you still have to inspect the car properly, but it's a great start. Any dealership should pay the cost of the CARFAX, and many private sellers will already have it available. You can use a resource like Kelly Blue Book (mentioned above) to get the projected value of the vehicle before you show up. Don't let the dealer tell you those prices aren't accurate, because they are. The prices from websites like KBB.com are based on actual numbers, and they're extremely current.

- **Don't coddle the seller's feelings.** Some people (especially kids) will be afraid to hurt the seller's feelings—whether private-party or dealership. Dealers will actually feed on this. It's great your children would care about others, but when it comes to a large purchase, they have to see it as a transaction. Don't ever let someone guilt your child into a purchase, and they sure will try.

When you show up to see the car your kid is interested in, it's time for a proper inspection. If the seller doesn't have the time for you to do this, then he doesn't have the time to sell you the car. Walk away. If you get a green light to inspect, start the following process:

## How to Inspect a Used Car

The best way to inspect a used car is to get permission to take it to a local mechanic you trust. Mechanics will inspect used cars for you—for cheap and sometimes free—so you know the car passes all the basic tests.

If you're left on your own to do the inspection, don't worry! You don't have to be an expert to help your kid inspect the car, you just have to look for a few key things. You can perform a full inspection right in front of the seller or car dealer.

**Inspection Checklist**

What you'll need to inspect the car:

1. A mirror
2. A magnet
3. A quarter
4. A dollar bill
5. A paper towel
6. A small flashlight
7. A USB/aux cord or CD

Use this 20-point inspection checklist:

1. **Overview.** Start by looking over the outside for any dents, scratches, or paint touchups. Use your mirror to look at the underside of the vehicle. Paint overspray is a sure sign of a body repair. A quick look down the side of the car, in the light, will show every little dent and ding. Make sure all pieces (e.g., hood, bumpers, fenders, etc.) have the same texture; if they don't, this is a sign of a paint job on all or part of the vehicle.
2. **Dollar Bill Trick.** Close each door (including the trunk/hatch) on a dollar bill. If you're unable to pull the dollar bill out, that's a good sign. If the dollar bill slips out of the closed door, that's a sign the car has

been wrecked, and something has been repaired or replaced.
3. **Rust Check.** Look for rust around and under the car. If one thing is rusted, it's likely there is more rust elsewhere.
4. **Windshield.** Look closely at the windshield for any chips or cracks. Depending on your state, you may have to repair these before it will pass inspection. Also look for cracks that appear to show small splits, which could turn into larger cracks.
5. **Wheels.** Check the wheels for any dents or bending. This is a sign the driver either hit a curb or a large pothole. It's not a dealbreaker, but you'll want to know if you have to replace the wheels down the road (ok, pun intended this time).
6. **Tires.** Check the tires for heavy wear or damage. Replacing tires is required maintenance, but if you'll need to replace them immediately, factor that into the price. You can use a quarter to check the tread. If you hold the coin upright, the tread should at least go to the bottom of Washington's head.
7. **Magnet Trick.** Use your magnet (ask permission first) to check for rust and filled areas. If the magnet doesn't stick to the metal parts of the car, that's a sign of a repair.
8. **Engine Noise Check.** Start the engine—preferably from a cold start—to listen for any unusual sounds. If there is any smoke, idle problems, or rattling, it may be best to avoid the car.
9. **Fluid Check.** It's time to look under the hood. Check the oil. If there isn't enough right now, the car has

likely been running with low oil, which is terrible for the engine. Make sure the oil is a golden color, not solid black (black oil is another sign the oil hasn't been changed in a while). Smell the oil. A burnt smell is a bad sign. Check the other fluids for proper amounts. As a bonus, you can always ask the seller if the blinker fluid has been changed recently. If he responds with anything other than, "blinker fluid isn't a thing," I wouldn't trust anything else he's told you about the car maintenance. That last point was just for fun, but you should try it. For amusement, if nothing else.

10. **Flashlight Test.** Use your flashlight to check for leaks, filth, and anything else that shows the car hasn't been properly taken care of. Check the battery and the terminals for corrosion. If the battery looks really old, a new one is something else to factor into the cost. If it looks like someone spilt their snow cone on the battery, you may need a new battery immediately.
11. **Smell Check.** Now hop into the car. Check the interior for signs of smoking or pets. The smell is usually a dead giveaway. You can also look for stains, ash, and cigarette burns.
12. **Lights.** Check the headlights, brake lights, tail lights, and all blinkers for proper function.
13. **Horn Test.** Check the horn for proper function.
14. **Seatbelt.** They should work properly, click into place, and lock appropriately.
15. **Heat & Air.** Make sure the heat and air conditioning work. It's common to only think about checking heat or air, based on the time of year. Check both. And don't forget to check the defrost. In our family's

history of cars, we've had to replace more than one blend door actuator (I didn't even know what that was until we replaced the first). This is a huge problem in the winter. So, don't forget to check the heat, even in the summer, and vice versa.

16. **Windows & Locks.** Check that all windows roll up and down, and all doors lock and unlock.
17. **Sound System.** Make sure the stereo works properly. Use your USB/aux cord or CD to test it. Turn the volume (and the bass) up to check for any blown speakers.
18. **Spare Tire.** Check for a spare tire and jack. Make sure all pieces are present for the jack. Put the jack on the ground to make sure it works… this will help to make sure all pieces are there.
19. **Key Fobs.** Test the key fob(s), if it comes with any, to make sure they work correctly (don't forget to check the panic button).
20. **Driving Test.** Now it's time to drive the car. Listen for any strange sounds. Briefly let the steering wheel go to see if the car blatantly veers to one side or the other (a sign an alignment is needed). Make sure the car shifts properly, especially if it's an automatic. A transmission is an *enormous* expense, and if you feel the car jump when shifting gears, that's not a good sign. If it's a manual transmission, make sure all gears work properly (including reverse!). You'd be surprised how many cars are missing an entire gear. A guy I used to work with didn't have first.

This checklist will get you through most of the headache involved in an inspection, if you can't take it to a mechanic.

When kids are young, a vehicle isn't always necessary. If you live in a larger city, public transportation is a great tool, as long as it's safe. Let's look at some transportation options that don't include a vehicle.

Transportation Without Buying a Car

A car isn't always a necessity. In more rural regions, it may be the only way, but that doesn't mean your children must own one. Don't feel bad if it's not possible—given your current financial situation—for your children to have a car. A family car is always a good option, especially if you have multiple kids starting to drive.

In more condensed areas, or large cities where you're close to everything, walking, biking, or scooting (scooters are becoming more popular globally) could be an option. A little exercise never hurt anyone. In larger metropolitan areas, public transportation is a great option. The most important concern here is safety.

Caring for the Car

When your teen begins their driving journey, they should know the basics of car care. Your kids will be driving around in a giant box of metal worth thousands of dollars. They can at least make sure the tires have enough air.

Your kids should know *how to*:

- Check the oil and other fluids, and add [the proper]

fluid when needed.
- Check the tire pressure, and add air when needed.
- Change any and all of the light bulbs.
- Jump start the car when needed.
- Replace the windshield wipers.
- Wash and wax the car.
- Replace the air filter.
- Change a tire.

Your children may want to eventually learn *how to*:

- Change the oil.
- Replace the brake pads.
- Replace the spark plugs.
- Replace the battery.

Your children don't have to be mechanics to drive a car, but they should at least know how to properly care for such an expensive luxury.

Summary - Transportation

**The Car-Poor Life**
Don't let your kids become car poor. Explain how this is a common pitfall, and how they can avoid it.

People are car-poor for three reasons:

1. They think car payments are [and will always be] part of life.

2. They are trying to impress others with what they drive or their identity is attached to the type of vehicle they own.
3. They want a nicer vehicle than they can afford, which means this vehicle is more important than having this amount of money for retirement or anything else.

Teach your children to have a healthy view of vehicle ownership.

**Paying for the Car**
Before you decide at what age your child should start driving, consider the financial and personal risk involved.

Decide who is going to pay for the car, insurance, and maintenance.

Don't co-sign for your child. If it already happened, review the section on what to do if you already co-signed.

**Finding a Great Deal on Your Kid's Car**
Remember, buying from a private party will almost always be cheaper than buying from a dealer. Dealers are, however, more convenient.

Follow these tips when your child is looking for a car:

- Don't let your kids get married to the car.
- Don't be afraid to walk away.
- Be informed from the start.
- Don't coddle the seller's feelings.

## SEVEN
# THE DEBT TRAP
#### RAISE DEBT-FREE-FOR-LIFE KIDS

"Never spend your money before you have it."

> THOMAS JEFFERSON, FOUNDING FATHER AND
> THIRD PRESIDENT OF THE UNITED STATES

"Some debts are fun when you are acquiring them, but none are fun when you set about retiring them."

> OGDEN NASH, AMERICAN POET

"Debt is normal. Be weird."

> DAVE RAMSEY, AUTHOR, BUSINESSMAN, AND RADIO SHOW HOST

Gone are the days when a mortgage was the only sizable debt taken on in life. Today, it's common to see car payments rival house payments. Just look back to the opening story in the previous chapter about Greg, who suddenly came into an $1,100 car payment.

In 2015, Standard & Poor conducted a financial literacy survey and found Americans are getting financially dumber. Financial literacy has been decreasing for decades, which could help explain why debt has been increasing.[1]

Americans now hold over $1 trillion in credit-card debt and over $13 trillion in total debt. The credit-card debt includes the total spent every month on credit cards, including the balances that are paid off in full. However, more than 60% of adults carry a balance from month to month.[2] Around half of the $1 trillion in credit-card debt is revolving debt. Auto loans are over $1 trillion as well, according to NerdWallet.[3]

The good news is, our kids don't have to fall into the debt trap.

### Don't Go Into Debt in the First Place

Let's be real, most Americans are broke. Seventy percent of Americans are in debt, and 50% think they always will be. Seventy-eight percent are living paycheck-to-paycheck and most don't have enough savings to cover even the smallest emergency.[4]

The first step to getting out of debt is: don't get into any more debt. If your children haven't left home yet, they're likely not in debt yet, so they can skip this step. That alone puts them ahead of most Americans. Skipping that one step, and not going into debt, could mean the difference between wealth and financial insecurity.

It's easy to not get into debt. It's much harder to dig your way out. It's possible for your children to never pay interest a day in their lives. It's easy, actually. All they have to do is refuse debt. Trust me, it's possible and sustainable to live a debt-free life. Refusing debt starts by refusing credit cards.

## The Psychology of Spending

I've been through many stages of thought on the "cash vs. credit" debate. I started by loving credit cards, and never paying them off at the end of the month. Then I read Dave Ramsey's books and cut up all of my credit cards. After I crawled out of debt, I started getting into credit-card rewards, and I went back to spending almost 100% on credit but paying it off each month to avoid paying any interest. Now I'm back to preferring cash over credit. Why? Well, studies began a few decades ago to look into the spending habits of people who use credit cards, compared with cash spenders. In 2001, Massachusetts Institute of Technology (MIT) did a study involving college students bidding on three different items. When the students were allowed to use credit cards, they spent between 80%-100% more than students using only cash.[5]

A decade later, a study in the Journal of Consumer Research gave some insight into why people spend more with credit than cash. It turns out, people tend to associate credit cards with the *benefits* of the product they're buying, yet they associate paying cash with the *cost* of the product.[6] This isn't by accident. It's mostly by marketing. We have the major credit-card companies to thank for that. But "benefits vs. cost" isn't the only reason we spend more with credit. Hal E. Hershfield, PhD explains that when we purchase on credit, we have more time to think about the purchase, between the time of the transaction and the time we actually pay the bill.[7]

Studies continue to confirm that we spend more with credit cards. From restaurant tips to auto tolls, we mindlessly spend more in every area, when we use a credit card.[8]

## Credit Card Rewards Vs. Overspending

I'm all for credit-card rewards, but given the studies above, I'm not so sure they're worth it. I still use credit cards, and get rewards from all of them, but I'm actually considering making a change. If nothing else, those studies helped me be more mindful with my purchases, and hopefully they've helped you do the same. These are the things our kids should know—things we would have loved to know earlier.

In his book, *Deep Work: Rules for Focused Success in a Distracted World*, Cal Newport, talks about the "any-benefit" of things. He explains how we tend to stick with things as long as they provide *any* benefit, but it's important to look at what provides the *most* benefit. I think it's plain to see, while credit cards do offer benefits, cash offers the greatest benefit by spending less money overall (factoring in rewards and all).

I am highly intentional with my spending. I stick strictly to a budget. Yet, I still believe I would spend less if I used cash. Cash is real. We *see it* leaving our pockets. Credit is more like pretend. We're chasing credit-card rewards, while spending way more than we otherwise would, and all too often, digging our way into a hole (i.e., the debt trap).

Even with an astronomically conservative estimate—taking

all above studies into account—we spend around 10% more when we use credit than when we use cash. Is that worth the 1%-5% cash back? I don't think so.

Perhaps we should encourage our kids to never get caught up in chasing credit-card rewards, and to stick with cash. That never opens the possibility of falling into heaps of credit-card debt. Why encourage credit for the *any-benefit*, when we could encourage cash for the *most* benefit?

## The Great Car-Payment Myth

Oh, car payments. Everyone has one, right? Well, actually, it seems like it's more of a poor and lower-middle-class thing—not because they have less money, but because they buy more car.

Car payments are getting higher, and car-payment terms are getting longer—up to an average of 66 months. On top of that, Americans are borrowing almost $1,000 more overall on the average loan.[9] Considering how many Americans are living paycheck-to-paycheck, this isn't a small problem.

In *The Millionaire Next Door: The Surprising Secrets of America's Wealthy*, Thomas J. Stanley, PhD explains how the average millionaire doesn't have a car payment, and he doesn't have a new car. It's typical for the average millionaire to drive a slightly used car and pay cash for it. But this isn't just for millionaires.

The only car payment your children ought to have is a payment to themselves, in an interest-bearing account. Once they buy their first car, they can start saving for the next car.

Even if they put the money into a savings account, bearing practically no interest, they'll still have $24,000 after five years of saving $400/month. That means zero interest paid and zero debt. If you instill this mindset before your children leave home, they'll never have a car payment in their life.

## How to Never Have a Mortgage

Mortgages are like car payments, but it's more understandable that you would need a loan for something that typically costs at least six figures. That doesn't mean anyone *needs* a mortgage. It's highly possible to buy a house without one.

The "American Dream," encourages us to buy a "starter home," when we are starting out as young adults. We are told we need to buy a home instead of renting. We are told renting is throwing our money away.

The truth is, renting is a necessary part of progressing through adulthood, and at no point do you ever *need* to buy a home. I'm not saying you, or your children, shouldn't buy a home. At some point, it's nice to have a home that belongs to you, that you can do whatever you want with, and that you don't owe someone else money for. But that doesn't have to take 30 years.

Remember, if you have to finance something, you can't afford it. Take that mentality into homeownership, and it doesn't seem like anyone can afford much. Here's the secret: you can't. Not when you're first starting out anyway. That's why it's called a "starter home." It shouldn't be much of a home. Not yet.

### The Trade-Up Approach to Home Buying

If your children start saving for their first home as soon as they move out, they can have enough to buy a starter home in about 10 years. That means renting, as inexpensively as possible, for 10 years, to pay 100% cash and 0% interest for their first home.

Mortgages cost more than we think. They often cost people two to three times the price of the home, over the mortgage term. It's perfectly fine for your kids to start with a small home they can actually afford. If your children refuse to go debt-free with their first home, encourage a maximum of a 15-year mortgage.

A standard $150,000 home, on a 30-year, fixed 3.9% interest rate (current standard rate), comes out to $104,700, in interest paid over the life of the loan. The same loan with a 15-year, fixed 3.6% interest rate (current standard rate—shorter loans usually have lower interest rates), comes out to $44,346, in interest paid over the life of the loan.

That's $60,354 less in interest payments, and you're not even making double-sized payments. The payment for that 30-year loan would be around $1,050, while the payment for a 15-year loan is $1,425. That's less than a $400/month difference to save over $60,000 and 15 years of your child's life.

A starter home should be just that: a beginning. It should be a home you can make a few improvements on and sell for a profit. Upgrade slightly with the next house and take the same approach into the next purchase. Home buying is about trading up until you get the dream home you want.

## Do You Really Need a Credit Score?

If you're living debt-free, why focus on a credit score? In reality, a credit score is a *debt score*. Take the FICO score, for example. The FICO is a type of credit score based on your overall credit report and credit history. This is how your FICO is determined:

- 35% payment history
- 30% amounts owed
- 15% length of credit history
- 10% credit mix
- 10% new credit

If your children never get into debt, they won't need a credit score.

Prior to writing this book, I did some research to find out the reasons our society is obsessed with credit scores. U.S. News & World Report gave five reasons:

1. Renting an apartment
2. Buying a home
3. Refinancing student loans
4. Getting a credit card
5. Getting your next job

The Balance gave five reasons as well (as a side note, I do appreciate that The Balance also wrote an article on living without debt and without a FICO score). Their reasons were similar, but they added three more:

1. Having a low car payment
2. Funding a small business
3. Utilities

Basically, those are eight different things that supposedly warrant a credit score. Let's address each one of these (I'll combine some for brevity):

- **Renting** – You don't need credit to rent an apartment or get your next job, you simply need references. Moreover, if you explain your debt-free lifestyle, that will typically intrigue the apartment manager or employer, and often set you apart from the competition (in a good way).
- **Financing** – If you don't use debt to finance your home, your degree, your business, or your car, you won't need a credit score. You'll just need actual money (remember that stuff?).
- **Utilities** – The only thing that may change when it comes to your utilities, if you don't have credit, is that you'll have to pay a deposit, which you will get back, because it's a deposit.
- **Credit Cards** – I'm not going to address the credit-card point. I think you get the idea.

If you can find one small thing that does require a credit score, I promise you it's not worth it. Look at the trade-off. Even if your children decide they want to take out a mortgage, they can use manual underwriting to prove their ability to pay back the money.

While having low credit can affect your children with things like job searching, utility payments, and business ownership, having *no credit* doesn't affect them in the same way. Having no credit often sparks curiosity in employers, and I've heard of people being called back in for a second interview because the employer was so curious about the applicant having no credit (and no debt). In the case I'm referring to, the person actually got the job partially because of the conversation on being debt-free. His boss felt it showed a sense of responsibility. Because it does.

## Debt-Free for Life

Your kids can win the debt fight; they don't even have to get in the ring. The four main areas where debt creeps into people's lives are credit cards, auto loans, mortgages, and the "need" for a credit score. We're about to get into the fifth way debt enters our life in the next chapter: college and student loans.

A debt-free lifestyle is radical and not widely accepted. It's hard to shift a paradigm that is so deeply woven into the fabric of America, but it can be done.

## Summary – The Debt Trap

**How to Raise Debt-Free-for-Life Children**
Living a debt-free life is different. Teach your children to live differently. If we teach kids how to stay out of debt, we won't be showing them how to dig their way out of later.

**The Psychology of Spending**
Studies show that we spend much more when we spend on credit… likely so much more that it negates any sort of credit-card rewards or benefits.

Credit cards were invented to make us spend more. Don't let your kids fall into the trap.

**Car Payments**

Car payments are not a necessary part of life, despite popular opinion.

**Mortgages**
Regardless of what society tells us, mortgages are not a requirement for a good life. Your children can buy their home with cash, if they rent and save first. If they decide to get a mortgage, prefer shorter terms to save thousands.

Consider the trade-up approach to home buying.

**Credit Scores**
A credit score is a debt score. If your children never plan on getting into debt, they don't need credit. You don't actually need a credit score to rent an apartment, buy a home, or get a job.

# EIGHT
# COLLEGE CONVERSATIONS
## GET A DEBT-FREE DEGREE

"Fathers send their sons to college either because they went to college or because they didn't."

    L. L. HENDERSON, U.S. CONGRESSMAN AND LAWYER

"Some people get an education without going to college. The rest get it after they get out."

    MARK TWAIN, AUTHOR AND EARLY ENTREPRENEUR

"Student debt is a product that has been sold to us with such repetition and intensity that most people believe they can't live without it."

    DAVE RAMSEY

CHRIS AND I GREW UP TOGETHER. He went to college for almost six years and didn't finish his four-year degree. A few years later, he went back and completed the last few classes. Nine years into his working life, he had finally received his degree in mass media and communications. What did he do with his degree? Does he work in marketing? Video? Radio? Nope. He's a manager at a local restaurant, because it paid substantially more than any job his degree would get him into. Sure, he could've worked his way up and earned more than the restaurant pays, but he had a family early on and needed the money. Honestly, he's doing great as a restaurant manager and he loves his job.

Why did he get a degree if he doesn't use it? Because he went to college for the sake of going to college—with no direction whatsoever. He had no plan, he just knew he "should" go to college. So many kids find themselves in the same situation today.

My friend Mike works as a consultant for a large tech company, earning six figures. He's self-taught, but the position required a degree. Fortunately for Mike, he has a degree. A degree in some technology major? Far from it. He has a four-year degree in Christian administration, from a non–accredited Christian college. The tech company wanted to see a degree—to see an ability to persevere and accomplish things. But they didn't care where the degree came from, or what the degree was in, for that matter.

What do these stories have in common? They both bust myths about college, from thinking of college as a requirement to overestimating the importance of where your degree comes from.

College can be valuable. It can also be insanely expensive. It may even be unnecessary. There are all kinds of questions surrounding college, and we're going to dive into the biggest ones to find some answers.

Should you pay for your children's education? Or is it their responsibility to pay their way?

What type of account should you use if you want to give them a head start?

Should they even go to college?

We're going to get into all of this, and you'll see all your options if you do decide to invest some money for their education. Let's start with the question you have to help them answer first: Should they even go to college?

## Is College a Requirement?

I don't think we ask ourselves these difficult questions enough.

A trend started back with the Baby Boomers: the idea that college would be the golden ticket to catapult their children into a better life. Financial success could only come from a college degree.

But college isn't for everyone. The mindset that college is the only path to success often pushes kids into useless degrees and mountains of debt. It can feel productive, but it can also be a form of procrastination, delaying you from joining the workforce for a few more years while you search for direction. It's an expensive way to "find direction."

The studies do seem to show the value of a college degree. The U.S. Census Bureau conducted a survey on earnings across a 40-year work life.[1] The median annual earnings for someone who didn't seek education after high school was only $1,371,000 over the 40 year period, while those with a bachelor's degree achieved $2,422,000 in earnings in the same timeframe. A master's degree earned $2,834,000 during that period, and a doctorate degree earned $3,525,000 over 40 years.

Likewise, a recent Georgetown University study showed, on average, college graduates earn around $1 million more over their lifetime than those without a degree.[2] Similarly, the Pew Research Center found there is roughly a $17,500 annual income-gap between those with a degree and those without, on average.[3] All of these studies seem to be pointing in the same direction.

However, there may be more to it.

These studies include all of the people who went to college for a specific reason. Pay special attention to the term "on average" in those studies. You don't have to go far to find studies, and even real-world examples, of people who are underemployed and simply not using their expensive degree (and likely never will). College is best used with a specific career path in mind. Yes, that career path may change (most majors do), but the desire to go to college should at least begin with a career option (or multiple options) that needs college.

If you want to become a doctor, lawyer, or professor go to college. If you want to work for someone else in a corporation (i.e., climb the corporate ladder), go to college. However, if you want to start your own business, college may or may not be the place for you. Business degrees aren't as useful as people think, and this is coming from someone with a business degree. When it comes to starting a business, you may get more out of reading a few books, written by people who have started the business you want to start, than you will out of a semester in college.

In addition, don't discredit trade, technical, and vocational schools. These schools don't seem to hold the merit they should, but they are often the answer to your children's desires, depending on what they want to do with their life. Mike Rowe, former host of the show, *Dirty Jobs*, offers a scholarship to help pay for these trade schools.[4] If you weren't aware, he's a big advocate for trade schools.

The point is, don't force your kids to go to college just because you think it means a better life for them. It could end up meaning a bunch of student loans with nothing to show for it but a piece of paper. Make an educated decision, with your children, without feeling like your child's life will be over if they don't attend a university. It's ultimately their decision, but you can be their guide.

## Should You Help Pay for College?

There's no rule (written or unwritten) saying you have to help your children pay for college. In fact, one could make the argument that you're helping your children more by allowing them to pay their own way. Laura Hamilton, a professor at the University of California, Merced, found that the more parents help with college financially, the lower the grades seem to be.[5]

We are raising our children to become adults who function in the real world. Part of that is learning the value of hard work. We have more appreciation for those things we have invested our time and money into. For example, we tend to take better care of a vehicle that was purchased rather than given. If someone has to work their way through college, the days are more *intentional*; partying the nights away seems less appealing.

To avoid the "I didn't pay for this, so I don't care" attitude, but to also lovingly let our kids know we want to help, we've decided to pay for part of our children's education. We don't intend to pay for all of it. In fact, our goal and hope is that we don't pay for all of it. This will also encourage our kids to seek out scholarships and put the work in to make it happen if they really want it.

When the time comes to decide on whether or not your child will go to college, I hope this next section serves as a resource should you decide to help them pay for it.

## Educational Account Options

There are five main tax-advantaged options to invest in for your children's college funds. For most people, one choice is blatantly better than the others, and it's not the same choice for everyone.

Here are your options:

### 1. 529 Plans

A 529 plan is a great tool to invest or save for your children's college. There's over $300 billion in assets under management across the 529 plans nationwide, and it's increasing dramatically each year. People are starting to realize tools like this exist.

*What is a 529 Plan?*

A 529 plan, known legally as a "qualified tuition program," is a tax-advantaged savings plan for future education expenses. Authorized by Section 529 of the Internal Revenue Code, these plans are sponsored by states, state agencies, and educational institutions. Additionally, Section 529A covers Qualified ABLE Programs (for those with disabilities and other limitations). We'll discuss these as well.

While 529 plans are handled by each state individually, that doesn't mean you must invest in your own state's plan. You're free to choose the state that offers you the most benefit, even if you've never lived in [or even been to] that state.

There are two types of 529 plans:

1. **Prepaid Tuition Plan** – You purchase units or credits at participating colleges or universities for future tuition.
2. **Education Savings Plan** – This lets you open an investment account to save for your child's qualified higher-education expenses. You can also save for elementary or secondary public, private, or religious school tuition with this option.

Prepaid tuition plans are meant to be used in specific, predetermined schools. Education savings plans are more flexible and can be used at practically any school.

It's important to note, "Prepaid tuition plans usually cannot be used to pay for future room and board at colleges and universities and do not allow you to prepay for tuition for elementary and secondary schools."[6] Prepaid tuition plans are sponsored by the specific college or private organization where the money will be used. However, with education savings plans, you can use your investments to pay for tuition, fees, room, board, computers, and more. Every state sponsors at least one type of 529 plan. Well, every state except Wyoming. Come on, Wyoming! Get with the [qualified tuition] program! Even Washington D.C. offers one.

If you're just looking to save for your children's college expenses, and you don't want to risk losing any money, then a standard savings account works fine. 529 plans are meant for investing—to grow your money, tax-free.

Within the 529 plans, there are different types of investment funds. One of the most widely used is age-based funds, which are more aggressive or more conservative based on the number of years before college.

That's the beauty of 529 plans: you can invest aggressively while your child is young, striving for larger gains, which leaves you investing less money overall. Then, you can gradually move the money into more conservative funds as your child approaches college age.

*529 Plan: Fees and Expenses*

The list of fees associated with either of the above-mentioned plans can be lengthy. These fees are to be expected, just like with mutual funds. The same is true with the party who receives the fees listed below, while some are given to the state sponsor, others are for the plan manager. Some fees you need to consider are:

- Enrollment/Application Fee
- Ongoing Administrative Fees
- Maintenance Fees
- Program Management Fees
- Asset Management Fees

Some states offer direct-sold education savings plans where you have the option to invest without paying the broker fees. It's also possible to have some of the fees waived if you keep a large balance, start an automatic contribution plan (which is usually required), or have residency in the state sponsoring the plan. Look to each state website for the specifics on these waivable fees.

*529 Plans: Taxes and Penalties*

529 plans are tax-deferred plans, which means you don't pay federal taxes on any capital gains you earn, *as long as the funds are used for qualified education expenses*. You typically won't pay state tax either, but it depends on the state you choose. The specific tax benefits are different from state to state, but most states will allow you to deduct your contributions from your state income tax. Moreover, some states offer matching grants for 529 plans, but these benefits may only apply to residents of that state.

You are subject to a 10% penalty on the investment gains if the funds are not used for what the fund is intended for: education. If the money isn't used for education, you'll also pay federal and state (if applicable) income tax on the gains. Up to $15,000 in annual contributions qualify for the annual gift-tax exclusion, so you won't pay taxes on that money. But it gets even better. You actually have the option to give up to $75,000 in one calendar year, and it will be treated as five years-worth of gifts for gift-tax purposes.

Here's the best part: if your children get a full scholarship to a university, you can take the full amount of the scholarship out of your 529 plan without a penalty, but you will pay taxes on your investment gains as earned income.[7] If your kids get a full ride, they may deserve the cash, but that's your call whether you give it to them or use it for something else. If your child decides not to go to college, you can switch the 529 plan to another child, or simply pull the money out and take the 10% hit, plus taxes on the gains.

*529 Plan: Circulars and Restrictions*

A 529 plan's *circular*—also referred to as a disclosure statement, disclosure document, program description, or offering document—is a document containing all the specifics you should know about the plan. You actually need to read this; it's not just useless fine print.

The circular will lay out all the restrictions specific to that plan. This could include restrictions on investment options, and potential penalties for things you didn't even know existed.

There are some restrictions that apply to all 529 plans. You usually only have a handful of investment options, and you'll only be able to switch how you invest twice per year (or if the beneficiary changes), under current tax law.

*529 Plans: K-12 Education*

One recent change is your ability to use 529 plans to fund grade school, such as private or religious schools, but practically any paid grade school qualifies. This applies federally to all 529 plans, but all states haven't adopted this on a state level, so you have to check your specific state's law.

There's a $10,000/year limit, per child. Your state's circular will explain more of the specific benefits and guidelines of their K-12 program. Of course, if you haven't started investing yet, you'll just need to find a state that allows the K-12 option. Using a 529 plan for K-12 education only makes sense in a few situations, since the money often won't have enough time to grow, which means it won't be worth your while to invest.

*529 Plans: Financial Aid*

529 plans do count as assets on most financial aid forms, and thus, they will generally affect the amount of aid your child is able to receive. The purpose of a 529 plan is to eliminate or reduce the amount of debt your child pays through student loans. Whether the assistance comes from the 529 plan or from financial aid, it all helps. But saving your own money is always more reliable than depending on financial aid programs.

*529 ABLE Accounts*

The ABLE (Achieving a Better Life Experience) Act, signed into law in December 2014, allows Americans living with disabilities to save for college and other expenses, as a supplement to insurance. Qualified expenses include, but are not limited to: education, job training, job support, healthcare, and financial management. It is a tax-deferred benefit, similar to standard 529 plans, but specifically for expenses associated with a disability.

Here are a few important things to know about ABLE accounts:

1. Before ABLE accounts existed, disabled Americans couldn't earn more than $700/month, or have more than $2,000 in assets, without the risk of forfeiting benefits from government programs like Medicaid.
2. Disabled Americans can have up to $100,000 in an

ABLE account and still be eligible for Supplemental Security Income (SSI) benefits; however, once they exceed that amount, they are no longer eligible to receive those benefits.
3. The PATH Act of 2015 removed residency requirements from ABLE accounts, giving disabled Americans the option to use any state's plan. Granted, there are still residency *benefits* like there are with many standard 529 plans.

To qualify for a 529 ABLE account, you must be diagnosed with a significant disability, expected to last a minimum of 12 consecutive months, before turning 26 years old. The disabled individual must be able to get a disability certification from his or her doctor or must be receiving SSI and/or SSDI benefits.

*Finding the Best 529 Plan*

So, you've decided a 529 plan is right for your child. How do you know which plan to choose? While a few states do offer special benefits for its residents, it pays to look across the country at all your choices. Finding a good 529 plan comes down to a few things:

- **Low expense ratio/fees** – A good expense ratio should be well under 1%, and many 529 plans are well below this.
- **Diverse investing options** – Look for a fund with lots of options, such as multiple asset-class and age-based options.

- **Tax deductions/benefits** – Usually reserved for in-state residents, tax benefits shouldn't be overlooked.
- **Your preferred options** – Whether you want the 529 plan to include real-estate investments, exchange-traded funds (ETFs), age-based funds, or simple index funds, find a fund that matches your desires. With all the options available, there's likely one that does.

The common denominator with any investment is low expenses and diverse options. Choose a plan that makes the most sense for your situation. Start with your state of residence and then check other states until you find the one you feel is the best fit.

Despite the fact that the last several pages were devoted to 529 plans, they aren't the only option. Let's finish this discussion with the pros and cons of 529 plans:

*529 Plan Pros:*

- You are in total control of the money.
- Your child has no control of the money.
- There are no income restrictions.
- Most states have no age limit to when the money has to be used.
- They are easily transferred to other children in the family.
- They can be used for trade and vocational schools.
- They can be used for a variety of expenses associated with college life.

*529 Plan Cons:*

- You have no direct control over investments in the plan.
- Investment funds are limited.
- Each state has its own set of rules, fees, and expenses.

## 2. Coverdell ESA

The Coverdell Educational Savings Account, often called the ESA (formerly the Education IRA), is another option for your child's college expenses. It's an option, but it may not be an enticing one.

ESAs have a low annual contribution limit of $2,000 per year, per child (as of 2020). They have income restrictions and age restrictions. Because of all this, ESAs can be overly restrictive. You must use the money within 30 days after the beneficiary turns 30, and the beneficiary must be under 18 while you're contributing to the plan (with some exceptions for certain disabilities). Also, you can't contribute to an ESA if you earn more than a certain income (around $100,000 for individuals, and $200,000 for married couples, annually, as of 2020).

On a positive note, you have many investment options with ESAs, including most stocks, bonds, and mutual funds. Like a 529 plan, you can use an ESA to pay for lower-level education, as well as college. This is an option, but 529 plans typically offer many more benefits than ESAs. Let's look at the pros and cons of an ESA:

*ESA Pros:*

- Your investment options are vast.

- You can use the money to pay for lower-level education.
- You can use the money to pay for a tutor of test-prep classes.
- You can easily transfer the money to another beneficiary.

*ESA Cons:*

- The contribution limit is low.
- There is an income limit.
- There are age restrictions.

## 3. Roth IRA

A Roth Individual Retirement Account, or Roth IRA, is a great retirement tool, but it can also be used for education. This is one of the few uses a Roth IRA offers, outside of retirement. Should you use a retirement account for your child's education? There are two views on this:

1. One view is, you *should* use a Roth IRA for your child's education, because if your child doesn't end up using the money, you can use it for retirement.
2. The other view is, you *should not* use a Roth IRA for your child's education, because most people are already unprepared for retirement.

The majority of Americans are severely underfunded for retirement,[8] and with a fairly low annual contribution limit, there isn't enough room to invest for retirement and college in the same account.

Which view is right? I would be cautious of using a Roth IRA for your children's education, but if you do, make sure your retirement is set up first. You don't want to fund their college just so they can turn around and fund your retirement. If you have another retirement option, like a 401(k), Thrift Savings Plan (TSP), Simplified Employee Pension IRA (SEP-IRA), or a company pension, you may have the flexibility to use a Roth IRA for your children's college. Let's look at the pros and cons:

*Roth IRA Pros:*

- You can use the money for retirement if your child doesn't need it.
- You have a wide range of investment options (practically anything you want).

*Roth IRA Cons:*

- You can't contribute as much to retirement since the overall contribution limits are low.

**4. Municipal Bonds**

Municipal bonds, also known as munis, are best used for those in high-income brackets. Sure, you won't pay taxes on your capital gains, so that's appealing, but that's also the case with the other options. The yield is typically low, at around a 3-4% average, but that beats a savings account.

You aren't forced to use municipal bonds for education, so

there is some flexibility there. While municipal bonds aren't a bad option, they don't really retain the benefits of other college savings avenues. They are safer, since they are bonds, but that's also the reason for a lower rate of return. Let's check their pros and cons:

*Municipal Bond Pros:*

- Your options for how you use the money are flexible.
- Bonds are a relatively safe investment.

*Municipal Bond Cons:*

- There is a low yield of 3-4% on average.
- They don't retain benefits of other college savings plans.
- You have limited investing options.

## 5. Custodial Accounts

The Uniform Gifts to Minors Act and Uniform Transfers to Minors Act allow you to designate your child as a trustee with custodial accounts. However, once the child turns 18 or 21 (depending on your state), they have full rein of how to spend the money. Ever read the Parable of the Prodigal Son (Luke 15:11-32)? I'm not sure it's best to give your child free rein of the money *you've* saved, especially when they're just out of high school, but that's up to you. Here are the pros and cons:

*Custodial Account Pros:*

- I don't see any pros over the other options, but I didn't want to leave this option out, because it is an option.

*Custodial Account Cons:*

- Again, have you ever read the Parable of the Prodigal Son?

**What's Best for You?**

If your child decides to go to college, and if you decide to help pay for it, you have plenty of options for investing. While the 529 plan is becoming the most popular, and it's the most appealing for the majority of people, another option could be better for you. Before we go on, I want to point out a few things that get overlooked:

1. If you decide to use the money for something other than education, you only pay the 10% penalty on your investment *gains*, not on your contributions. Therefore, depending on the amount you've saved, it's often not that big of a deal if you end up using the money for something else.
2. Prepaid tuition plans are only a good idea if your child is planning to attend a specific college from the start. But even then, you may want to evaluate whether your children will have a say in where they go to college, if you've already decided the school for them, and prepaid the tuition.
3. You should pay attention to the signals your kids are

sending as to whether or not they want to go to college. You may want to cut the cord on college savings if your child has a plan in place that leaves college out of the equation.

4. You don't have to use any sort of a "college investment fund" to save for your child's college, regardless of how much the financial industry pushes these types of savings plans. For example, don't blindly start throwing your money into a 529 plan. You should never invest in something you don't understand. If you don't have a good reason for using a 529 plan instead of a regular savings account, a savings account may be the better option.

5. Nowadays, it seems like all parents are saving for their children's education... at least, that's how social media and financial institutions make it seem. The fact is, only 36% of middle-income families, and 29% of low-income families, have set aside *any* money for their children's college education.[9] It's ultimately your call whether or not you save for your children's college, and saving for college is not a requirement to be a good parent.

Whichever option you choose, the important thing is keeping this degree debt-free.

### How to Get a Debt-Free Degree

Student loans aren't a necessity. It's actually fairly easy to go to school without going into debt. Here's how to get the degree without the debt:

1. **Save for college** – You can use any one of the options above to save for your children's education. Whether you plan to help or not, *they* can still save. Their teenage years are an ideal time to work up some savings for school. If they know they're going to college, why wait until they graduate high school to consider the costs?
2. **Choose an affordable college** – There's no reason to cross state lines for school. Your local community college may be all your kids need. At a minimum, once you confirm the credits transfer to your child's college of choice, get the core classes knocked out at a lower-cost community college. Contrary to popular belief, few employers actually care about where your degree comes from; if they have the degree requirement, they just care that you have a degree.[10]
3. **Apply for scholarships** – If your child chooses not to work, or not to save for college, they can at least apply for scholarships. This can be a full-time job. It's best to set a goal, like two a day. If your child applies for two scholarships a day, for their entire senior year of high school (even just 3-5 days a week), they'll not only get better at writing papers, they'll see a nice return on their investment (investing time, receiving money).
4. **Work through college** – If your child doesn't have savings for school, and they don't have enough scholarships to cover the costs, it won't hurt them to work their way through college. The benefit to working through college is actually threefold: 1) working while in college tends to keep kids away from an unproductive lifestyle, 2) students who work

through college tend to put more energy into their studies, and 3) students who work part-time (not full-time) have better grades, according to *multiple studies*.[11]

5. **Join the military** – Obviously, this option isn't for everyone. But between Military Tuition Assistance (Military TA), and the GI Bill, you can have an entire degree paid for by the U.S. military. You'd be surprised how many people join purely for the educational benefits.

It turns out, "everyone has student loans," is another myth. And just because a lot of people have them, that doesn't mean your children have to. It's actually easy to get a debt-free degree. Much easier than it is to devote a lifetime to student loan payments.

Summary – College Conversations

Don't get caught up in the traditional view that college is for everyone. Be intentional about helping your children with this decision. It's ultimately up to them.

It's not our responsibility, as parents, to pay for our children's college education. It is an expression of generosity if we do decide to help.

**Educational Account Options**
The five basic options you have for education-specific investing:

1. 529 Plans
2. Coverdell ESA
3. Roth IRA
4. Municipal bonds
5. Custodial accounts

529 Plans work for the majority of people who want to help invest for their children's college, but it's not the option for everyone.

**How to Get a Debt-Free Degree**

Your children don't have to live with student loans. There are alternative ways to fund college:

1. Save for college.
2. Choose an affordable college.
3. Apply for scholarships.
4. Work through college.
5. Join the military.

NINE

# INVESTING

THE IMPORTANCE OF STARTING YOUNG

"I wish I had started investing at a younger age."

PRACTICALLY EVERYBODY

"Wealthy people invest first and spend what's left and broke people spend first and invest what's left."

ANONYMOUS

"Investing should be more like watching paint dry or watching grass grow. If you want excitement, take $800 and go to Las Vegas."

PAUL SAMUELSON, AMERICAN ECONOMIST AND FIRST AMERICAN TO WIN THE NOBEL MEMORIAL PRIZE IN ECONOMIC SCIENCES

Smarter, not harder. That's the goal, right?

With investing, "smarter" can mean a lot of things, but one of the easiest and most rewarding ways to invest smarter is to invest younger. Investing early in life practically guarantees financial freedom later in life.

I'm not a fan of the stereotypical American model of retirement (retiring to stop working and live life like a vacation). I think retirement is about freedom, but we'll talk more about this in a moment. Kids will typically invest similarly to how their parents invest. That means if you don't invest, well, there's a good chance they won't either. Whether your kids choose to invest in stocks, bonds, real estate, businesses, commodities, peer-to-peer lending, or inventions, starting young will increase their chances of success.

We're going to start this chapter off with eight reasons it's so important for your children to start investing as early as possible. I want you to see how powerful it is to get your kids on the right track now. It doesn't take much knowledge or effort on your part, but it will require some action.

**1. Compound Interest**

Do you understand how compound interest works yet? We've already covered it, but just to make sure you understand it before you bring the concept up to your kids, let's do a little recap. The simplest explanation you can give your kids is this: compound interest is "interest on interest." Interesting isn't it? You need to understand it to explain it, but don't worry, it's a simple concept.

Pop quiz! Let's see if you were paying attention when we talked about compound interest earlier. If you made a single investment of $1,000, with an annual interest rate of 10%, how much money would you have in 10 years (compounding annually)? If you said $1,100, you'd be wrong. If you said $2,000, you'd still be wrong. Those are the two most common answers I hear.

So how much would you have? $2,593.74.

If you understand why, skip to the next point. If not, let me explain. You may be forgetting one simple fact: at the end of the first year, you would have a total of $1,100 with the 10% interest added in. That means you'd earn 10% of $1,100 in the second year, and so on. As your money grows, you earn interest on the total amount, including the interest already earned.

See? Simple.

**2. Immediate Experience**

While 80% of parents believe it's important to talk to their kids about money, 71% of parents are reluctant to do so, according to a T. Rowe Price survey.[1] I didn't know a thing about investing until I hit my mid-20s. If I would've started getting investing experience through both learning and trial and error, my net worth could easily be triple what it is now.

The more your children learn now, the more years they have to put this experience into action. Money isn't the only thing that compounds. Investing at a young age will give your children compounded *experience*. Experience often translates to mistakes. Mark Twain said it best: "Good decisions come from experience and experience comes from bad decisions." Mistakes are ok if they teach a lesson.

### 3. Recover From Mistakes

When you invest early on, time is on your side. If your children start investing in their teens, they will have plenty of time to make plenty of mistakes with their money. And we all make plenty of mistakes with our money. Financial mistakes can be devastating. Let's not forget, a 50% loss completely offsets a 100% gain. Money mistakes hurt. But they hurt less when you're young.

Making these mistakes at 18 or 20 years old gives your children plenty of time to get back on the horse (bull?—the lame investing jokes are included in the price of this book). They may totally screw up, invest poorly, and lose all of their money, but they have so many years left to recover, and with much more experience.

### 4. Take More Risks

The higher the risk, the higher the potential gain.

Some people start investing so late they virtually can't take any risks. When your children start investing early, they can take all the risks! Well, maybe not *all* the risks, but many more than someone who's late to the game.

It's true that the best time to start investing was 20 years ago, but the second best time to start is today. It's always the right answer to start earlier.

You may be the one who wishes you started investing 20 years ago. Since we can't go back in time as far as I know (I'm still working on it), we can at least help our children to not make our mistakes.

## 5. More Organized Finances

As a Christian, you are to give your "first fruits" to God, but the second helping should go to yourself. If your children automatically deduct giving, investing, and saving, before other expenses, this leaves them with an organized place to arrange a high-functioning budget. When they get this concept as children, organized finances will come naturally in adulthood.

## 6. Discover Preferences

Your children can *discover* the style of investing they prefer. Figuring this out at a young age means more time to do the investing they prefer.

They could take a huge hit in the stock market when they're young, and decide they prefer the stability of real estate. They may discover investing tools that make it easy and fun. If your children decide to invest in rental property, and begin to save for their first investment home at 18, they could own a full portfolio by the time they're in their early 40s.

## 7. Less Money is Required

With an IRA, there's something called "catch-up contributions." For people 50 and older, they're allowed to contribute an additional $1,000/year just to catch up on their retirement contributions. The government understands those individuals need to contribute more money than your 20-year-old son, because they didn't get the same head start.

In a study done by Grow Your Capital (GYC), they used the example of a 20-year-old who would need to save a mere

$158/month for 40 years to have a million dollars at age 60 (assuming a 10% rate of return). Over the 40 years, he would only contribute $76,000 of his own money. Comparing this to someone who is 40, the monthly amount would be $1,317, for a total of $316,000 in contributions to reach the same million dollar goal by age 60.[2]

When your children start investing young, *compound interest* and *time* will contribute more to their retirement than they will. That's the point behind all of this! The younger you start, the less you have to contribute.

When you add up these seven points, the result is #8.

## 8. Retire Young

Now for the event you've all been waiting for. Just like how all roads lead to Rome,[3] all of the above points lead to early retirement. Like I said in the beginning, I'm not talking about the retirement most people imagine.

Retirement, as a government concept, was adopted by countries during the late 19th century, and the early 20th century.[4] It's a concept that was created and has been sensationalized over the last century (Censationalized? See what I did there?). When the retirement concept first came on the scene, people were retiring with a few years of life left, to live those years out in peace. With people now living much longer and retiring earlier, retirement often means 20 to 40 years of "peace." That wasn't the original intent.

Retirement should mean financial freedom, not quitting work and doing nothing with your life. You have built financial freedom and retired early so you could enjoy those years of freedom to follow your calling or follow through with your passion!

Retirement is the goal because it puts you in control of how you spend your time, not because it means you no longer work. I think it's God's intent that we will always productively contribute to society. I don't believe we "deserve" to stop working just because our nest egg reaches a certain size, or we reach a certain age. We should raise our children to understand that work isn't a bad thing.

People who stop working entirely won't have to worry about many retirement years, because they won't last that long. That's the hard truth. When people stop doing, people stop being. They just fade away, and their health goes with their actions.

The stereotypical American view of retirement is slothful and wasteful. Encourage your kids to start investing early on in life to create *productive, meaningful* retirement years. Of course, it's their choice how they spend those years, but encourage them to do something big for the Kingdom of God and others in those years. Early investing makes that possible.

## How to Teach Your Kids to Invest

Investing isn't something we're taught in school. There would be too much disagreement over it to implement any sort of curriculum.

If you don't feel qualified to teach your kids about investing, you're not alone, but you're also not incapable. It's not hard to teach them investing concepts that will change their life. Concepts you weren't privy to. Simple concepts.

It just takes a few ideas to make your kids financially unstoppable.

## Teach Saving, Then Investing

Investing isn't the first step, it's the finish line. Before you get into stocks, mutual funds, and index funds, your children need to simply understand some money is for now, and some is for later. That's where *saving* comes in. You know the classic "give, save, spend" jars. We've already talked about them a little. They work because it is a visual example of delayed gratification.

Remember, when your kids are young, they need to see that big clear jar filling up with dollar bills. They need to get the concept of not spending everything they receive, and the concept of watching that saved money grow over time. Part of everything they ever receive goes to "give" and part to "save." Later on, you can add that "grow" jar for investing.

Slowly work up from savings accounts to conservative investments. Things you may never consider as an adult, like a Certificate of Deposit (CD). This way kids learn how interest works, which we'll talk more about in a moment (as if we haven't talked about it enough… well, we haven't!). If your children put $100 into a CD, and then receive $103, years later, they'll understand they earned money by not touching the money—by waiting. The goal isn't to make huge gains in the beginning, it's to teach the concept of "invest, wait, earn."

Another option is a conservative mutual fund. You want your children to invest in something that will move up or down, but not by much. I'll explain why below. Regardless of which option you choose, the important thing is for your children to know this: pay yourself first.

## "Pay Yourself First"

Again, "pay yourself first," is just the name of a concept. While we technically pay God first, and then ourselves (invest, saving, etc.), it's important to implement this idea of "pay yourself first" to remind your kids to invest and save before budgeting monthly expenses. The only way investing and saving actually happen is to "pay yourself first." As adults, we realize that if we wait until the end of a paycheck to invest, there won't be anything left to invest. Adults will often agree this is the most logical way to invest, but fail to follow through.

Starting your kids off with the pay-yourself-first mindset, will allow them to effortlessly become disciplined with their long-term investments. The younger you start, the better. Compound interest... compounds. We've already covered this... a few times. I just want to stress it, since 66% of Americans still don't understand how compound interest works, according to a study from The George Washington School of Business.[5]

What Not to Do

I don't want to insult your intelligence, so I will assume you've read an article or two and you realize any opinion piece can be applied differently to different people. My goal is to tell you what I have learned in my years of experience in both having children and teaching children about investing.

It's common advice to let your child buy a share of Disney (that seems to be the go-to when talking about kids), or some other company they can relate to. The idea is that they will understand how stocks work. Well, kids are actually capable of understanding how stocks work with a brief explanation, but that doesn't mean you should let your 10-year-old buy stocks.

I suggest more conservative methods when you're first

teaching your kids to invest, and I don't just say this because there is less of a chance of losing the money. I say this because there's less of a chance of anything happening—in either direction.

When your child buys that Disney stock, and the price skyrockets, they're pretty sure they did that all on their own. They think they must be a great investor. They're going to be the next Peter Lynch. They can do no wrong. And what about the opposite? When Disney tanks, they decide maybe investing isn't for them. They're not good at it, and they should just quit while they're not too far behind.

Either way, your child learns nothing. If you want to show them how stocks work, simply… show them how stocks work. Your kids don't need to have skin in the game to get the lesson. On top of that, most of the time when people buy stocks for their child, their kid isn't even seeing the transaction go down. I chock this entire idea—buying your kid individual stocks—up to another case of great intentions and little actual learning value.

### It Doesn't Take Much

Unless your kids are planning to devote most of their waking hours to researching investments, simple index funds (if you remember from previous chapters, these are also known as passive funds) are all they need. Even Warren Buffett suggests, for the average person who isn't a professional investor, index funds are their best bet. Based on history, I'd say most professional investors would be better off if they'd taken the same advice, and stuck with index funds.

It's easy when you learn this stuff at 11 or 12 years old. That's why most investing books are written as if you're already behind and trying to catch up— because you didn't start at 11 or 12.

There are methods that work better than others and some methods that are proven over and over to not work at all. For example, spending 30 minutes a month reviewing some random individual stocks and buying whatever feels right at the time. That method seems to be one of the most popular, though I doubt anyone would describe it as a good idea.

The fact is, if you teach your kids to invest in index funds from a young age, your kids will do well financially. There's plenty of time to get them interested in other methods of investing, while using index funds all the while. Think of index funds as the foundation. Everything else is building up from there.

There's not that much to investing on a basic level. Contribute a portion of every dollar you earn to a range of low-fee index funds and the money will grow. A small amount each month, over a lifetime, will yield huge results. The important thing is taking action and starting as soon as possible.

We've already discussed how important mindset is in all of this. It's actually so important that the second half of this book is entirely about mindset. We're not totally finished talking about money, but it *all* comes back to mindset. I'd argue the second half of this book may be more important than the first. It's time to get into your head, and into your child's head… in a good way.

Summary - Investing

**How to Teach Investing to Children**

Investing should be smarter, not harder. Simplicity wins the game.

It's vital for your children to start investing at a young age for eight reasons:

1. They take advantage of compound interest.
2. They will gain immediate experience.
3. They have time to recover from mistakes.
4. They are able to take more risks.
5. They will have more organized finances.
6. They can discover their preferences.
7. They will spend less money over time.
8. They can retire young.

Teach your children to save first to get the concept. Then teach investing.

Instill the pay-yourself-first mindset. Teach your children to give, save/invest, and then spend.

**What Not to Do**
Don't automatically buy stocks for your children. It can be a dangerous game, especially starting so young. If they do well, they'll think they're experts. If they do poorly, it could scare them away from investing entirely.

**It Doesn't Take Much**
If your children start investing early, financial freedom will be easy.

# PART TWO
# MINDSET

## TEN
# INTENTIONAL OWNERSHIP
### SHIFT TO PRACTICAL MINIMALISM

"Simplicity is the ultimate sophistication."

LEONARDO DA VINCI, ARTIST, INVENTOR, THINKER,<br>AND OFTEN CONSIDERED A "UNIVERSAL GENIUS"

"It is preoccupation with possession, more than anything else, that prevents men from living freely and nobly."

BERTRAND RUSSELL, BRITISH PHILOSOPHER,<br>LOGICIAN, AND WELL-ROUNDED ACADEMIC

"The secret of happiness, you see, is not found in seeking more, but in developing the capacity to enjoy less."

SOCRATES, A FOUNDER OF WESTERN PHILOSOPHY

One thing I appreciate about moving companies is, they do all the work for you. From packing your home into boxes to loading it on the truck, and even putting it all away in your new home if you want. Something I don't appreciate about moving companies is, they tell you exactly how much weight you have. While I could do without knowing that, it is eye opening. We saw our weight increase from 11,000lbs to almost 14,000lbs in four years. Yes, we have five kids, but 14,000lbs? We all acquire more things as our families grow, and while many of those things are necessities, much of it is acquired by pure consumerism. So many of the financial problems people face are created by consumerism.

When we first moved overseas, we were each allowed two carry-on bags and two checked bags, like most flights. As a family of six at the time, we brought a total of 16 bags. Our youngest wasn't capable of carrying much back then, so it was up to the five of us to carry all the bags, and at many times to carry our youngest too (in a heavy car seat).

In contrast, last year we took a trip to Ireland, for two weeks, with one carry-on each, and one checked bag for the entire family. We're lighter as a family these days. Not only do we live lighter, with much less than 14,000lbs now, but we travel lighter. For a comprehensive guide to light travel with kids, go to FreedomSprout.com and type "travel" in the search box.

Life is easier with less stuff. The average American home has 300,000 items in it.[1] We have so much stuff that one in ten Americans are renting a storage unit to house the overflow of stuff they own.[2]

Our family has been on the minimalism journey for several years now. It's a process. That's why we take a self-imposed minimalist challenge each year to rid our home of 5,000 things. I hope we aren't able to do this challenge forever, but we've been doing it for a few years. Actually, 5,000 things doesn't seem like much, given the figure above.

If getting rid of 5,000 things piques your interest, you might just be a minimalist in the making.

We're going to discuss lifestyle, minimalism, and intentional living. My goal isn't to convert you into a minimalist; my goal is to help you see areas of your life you aren't living intentionally in. Intentional living is what this book is all about, from the first page to the last. It's about why we do what we do, and most importantly, actually knowing *why* and *what* we do.

Before we dive into what it means to be a minimalist, let's talk about what minimalism isn't. I don't want you to think this book just shifted into some sort of crunchy-granola manifesto. It's all related.

## What Minimalism is Not

Minimalism is not getting rid of everything you own. It doesn't mean your house should look like a staged magazine photo. It doesn't mean living in a tiny home… unless you want to. As a side note, I love the idea of tiny homes, but we have a few too many tiny humans living in our home to make that work at this stage of life. Finally, it's not about never buying anything again, including food, and thus, eating out of dumpsters. That's Freeganism. No judgment here, but that's not what this book is about. Though, if you have time, you should look up Freeganism. It's not for me, but it's really interesting, and I'll admit, a little weird.

When I mention the word "minimalism" to people, I usually get one of a few responses. They either joke about how having five kids isn't very "minimal." Or they'll say, "so you just don't own anything?" But what's becoming a more common response is, people are actually interested in doing it themselves.

It typically makes people feel better once they realize we do own stuff, and our house isn't as empty as they assumed. Nor is everything always in its place, neat, and orderly. We're minimalist humans, not minimalist robots.

In fact, our home is still quite cluttered as far as we are concerned. Minimalism is an ongoing process to reduce. It's not a quick change. That's why the popular minimalist blogger, Joshua Becker, named his blog, "*Becoming* Minimalist."

### What Minimalism Is

You can capture the concept of minimalism in two words: *intentional ownership*. That's how I define it. It really has little to do with the actual number of things you own, and everything to do with the reason you own them. It's being intentional about every single thing you bring into your home. If you want to take it a step further, minimalism carries over into every area of your life. Being intentional with your things, resources, time, relationships… everything.

It's about cutting what you don't need and keeping what you do, across the spectrum of your life.

Minimalism is by no means a new concept. In fact, it dates back at least 2,000 years.

Jesus was a minimalist before it was cool.

> "And Jesus said to him, 'Foxes have holes, and birds of the air have nests, but the Son of Man has nowhere to lay his head.'"

MATTHEW 8:20

The label "minimalist" is not what's important. Labels themselves are rarely important. Think about your walk with God; the label, "Christian," isn't important in itself. You can refer to yourself as a Christ Follower, Jesus Freak, New Jew or whatever else you can think up—the label doesn't matter. I wouldn't recommend "New Jew" though... that can be off-putting.

Whether you call yourself a minimalist or not, owning less will give you a greater chance of focusing on what truly matters. But calling yourself a minimalist, and then living a life of over-consumption, won't help you much either.

When Jesus was crucified, he had a handful of material possessions, and he could carry everything he owned on his person. We all know Jesus didn't focus on material possessions. That's no secret. So, should we follow in Jesus's footsteps and sell everything we own? Yes! I'm kidding... no that's not necessary. Unless you feel compelled to do so. In that case, go for it, you New Jew!

**Possessions and Judgement**

It's not wrong to own things. It's not wrong to have material possessions. And no one wants to get into a debate over how much or how little we should own.

The Christian with a $100k house may criticize the Christian with a $200k house. Yet, how does the third-world Christian view both of them, as he's living in his mud hut? In my experience, the third individual is probably the least critical of others, though in this debate, he would have the most room for bragging.

There will always be people with more than you and people with less than you. There's no magic number. We can't say, "well, once you own a house worth more than $200k, you're materialistic," or, "if you own a shirt worth more than $50, you're too caught up in your possessions!" What if I own a $49 shirt? Whew, I'm in the clear. The point is, there's no hard line or magic number. We're called to worry about ourselves, not others.

If there is such a metaphorical line that determines when you own too much, it's when your material possessions affect your relationship with God and/or others. The person with a $200k house, who goes into their fancy study, and reads their Bible every morning, could have a much closer relationship with God than the homeless Christian who judges other people for owning so many possessions.

I've met rich people who were truly generous and showed a Christ-like love for others. I've met poor people who judged everyone who had more than they had. It's not about your stuff, it's about your heart.

## Minimalist Heart Vs. Minimalist Home

The heart of the matter is contentment. It isn't about getting rid of stuff or living with less. It's about *wanting less* and being able to model contentment for your kids. Minimalism is a mindset, but it won't make you happy on its own.

Consumerism is a disease in America, thanks to the advertising and marketing we're surrounded with from birth. Breaking free from this bondage starts with a change of heart first and foremost, and then it flows over into a simpler life, and ultimately, a reduction in how much stuff we own. When you live intentionally, you fix your gaze on what truly matters. Things like people, experiences, life, making memories and not on, well... stuff.

## Our Minimalism Journey

We were in the process of slowly downsizing all of our belongings when we moved to Europe. It turns out, Europeans don't own as much stuff as Americans. Surprise, surprise.

What did this mean for us? It meant we went from a 2,200 sq ft house to an 1,100 sq ft house. This was a problem, because we still had 2,200 sq ft worth of stuff. We liked the idea of being forced to downsize. We were uncomfortable until we did.

On top of that, it's not easy to get rid of stuff in Italy, where we live now. In the States, there are thrift stores that will come pick up the stuff you no longer want, as well as many other avenues for donating and selling your things. In Italy, it's a challenge just to get rid of an old television. Not only are there fewer places to donate here, but recycling laws make it almost impossible to throw some things away. So, we've had to be creative and downsize even more slowly.

I had always preached that minimalism was easiest when you forced it by moving into a smaller home. However, we still did it slowly to avoid a burnout. Now I can attest that it's definitely more effective this way—the "forced" way—but I don't know if I would say it's easier. Regardless, it works.

### How You Can Start Minimizing

We've been on a journey to own less for years, and we buy less now than we ever have. We really have found we're happier as we own less. So how do you start?

The first step of minimalism is to emotionally detach yourself. This is also the hardest step. Once you do this, not only will it be easier to get rid of things, but you'll see how unimportant things really are.

We have to realize our memories aren't held in the things themselves. What's the point of keeping that old lamp your grandmother gave you 15 years ago? Yes, she has passed away and you loved her dearly, but that lamp has nothing to do with your relationship. You'll remember her without the lamp. It's not the object that holds the memory.

Before we dive into minimalism, here are three starting points:

1. **Get rid of your storage unit.** Whether it's your garage or an actual paid storage unit, you don't need it. Odds are, you haven't touched that stuff in over a year. Let it go.
2. **Get rid of your distractions.** It could be video games, movies, or computer programs. Get rid of the things that take away from the more important things. This could include your TV.
3. **Get rid of your excess.** The books you don't read and won't read again, the clothes you know you'll never wear. Whatever it is, get rid of what you no longer need. This could even include your car if you live in a city with decent public transportation.

Those are some big rocks; it gets more difficult with the small pebbles. You know some things you can blatantly do without, but when it comes to the rest of it, you must go slowly. Set a realistic goal and go for it. Use your initial motivation to drive you, and then stick to a consistent habit of decluttering.

I keep track of the things we get rid of with an app. Each time we get rid of something, I open the app and update the total count. I have a daily reminder to declutter. A notepad (physical or digital) works just fine. Or make it fun and in-your-face by writing the number on a small white board in a place you see every day. That serves as a great reminder.

## How to Stay Motivated

You'll have a lot of motivation in the beginning, and it may start to trail off. Seeing your progress over time will serve as a great motivator, but sometimes you need more. We've used these five tactics to keep the motivation strong:

1. **Read books on minimalism** – I read constantly (physical books, ebooks, and audiobooks). About once a month, I will read or listen to a book on minimalism, decluttering, or living simply. With each book, I'm more motivated to continue the journey. If a book a month is too much, make it an article a month. Or try a minimalist podcast to stay motivated.
2. **Talk about it often** – My wife and I have many conversations about why we're minimizing (with each other and with the kids), and about how we could do it better. Keep the idea fresh and the process steady.
3. **Put up reminders** – Put reminders in places you see

often to remind yourself you're in the process of minimizing, and especially *why* you're minimizing.
4. **Watch documentaries on minimalism** – My favorite is the one The Minimalists created: *Minimalism: A Documentary About the Important Things*. Find some more motivating documentaries.
5. **Don't overwhelm yourself** – Taking it slowly is the best path to success here. If you donate 5,000 things in one weekend, that may work for you. If it overwhelms you, take a step back and slow down. Remember, just 100 things a week will surpass the 5,000-item goal by the end of one year.

Get your kids in on this too. Don't donate their things for them; let them be part of the process. When it comes to kids, toys are a big-ticket item here. They need fewer toys than they think.

Summary – Intentional Ownership

**Shift to Practical Minimalism**
Most Americans own too many things. Teach your children to value the important things, instead of material possessions.

Minimalism is best defined as "intentional ownership."

**Possessions and Judgement**
It's not wrong to have material possessions, but we don't want our children to idolize possessions either.

There will always be people with more and less than us. We can only judge our own view of material objects.

**Minimalist Heart Vs. Minimalist Home**
Minimalism is a mindset.

The goal is to raise children with a heart to want less and be content with what they have.

**How You Can Start Minimizing**

- Get rid of your storage unit.
- Get rid of distractions.
- Get rid of your excess.

**How to Stay Motivated**

- Read books on minimalism.
- Talk about it often.
- Put up reminders.
- Watch documentaries on minimalism.
- Don't overwhelm yourself.

ELEVEN

## THE TOY TRAP

HOW FEWER TOYS LEAD TO HAPPIER KIDS

"Give children toys that are powered by their imagination, not by batteries."

H. JACKSON BROWN, FROM *THE COMPLETE LIFE'S LITTLE INSTRUCTION BOOK*

"We know experiences are more gratifying than objects, so it can be much more meaningful than adding more toys to the pile."

EMILY EDLYNN, CLINICAL PSYCHOLOGIST AND FOUNDER OF THE ART & SCIENCE OF MOM

"Limit the toys and games to a very minimal amount. Don't worry—you are not depriving your children. Really, you are giving them freedom ... This doesn't mean we're going to take all the toys away—it means they'll have less physical toys, but more imagination."

RACHEL JONES, FOUNDER OF NOURISHING MINIMALISM

---

For three months out of the year, Friedrich-Engels-Bogen, a nursery in Munich, Germany, takes away all of their kids' toys and leaves them with only tables, chairs, and a few blankets to play with.[1] At first, this may seem cruel, but on second glance, it's proven to be an effective way to encourage children to make their own fun.

It works.

Though this nursery only takes away all the toys for a quarter of the year, it's been an eye-opening look into the minds and creativity of children.

Gisela Marti, a teacher at the nursery, said:

*"In these three months we offer the children space and time to get to know themselves and because they are not being directed by teachers or toys, the children have to find new ways to master their day in their own individual way."*

The first day of this experiment proved to be a little boring for the children. They didn't know what to do, so they just sat around and stared at each other for much of the day.

Another teacher at the nursery, Gudrun Huber, said:

*"The children didn't know what to do, but we left them alone, even if they were bored, because sometimes things in life are boring and you have to learn to cope."*

The nursery workers stayed back to allow the children to do whatever they wanted. And by the second day, that's exactly what the children did.

Gudrun went on to say, "once the children realized they could do what they liked and they were in control, they really went a bit mad—they got very boisterous and excited, climbing all over the furniture." The children began laughing and playing with everything they did have... making forts out of blankets and creating their own games.

The Friedrich-Engels-Bogen nursery isn't the only nursery doing this across Germany, and the idea is starting to catch on around the world.

## We Appreciate More With Less

Does the story above mean you should donate all of the toys in your home? Probably not, but I'm sure it would be fine if you did. We all appreciate the things we have more when we have fewer things. When we can reach a state of contentment with, and an appreciation for, the things we have, not only will we be happier in general, but we won't want as many things.

It's not just about happiness. Your children will learn to be more creative and more sociable when there are fewer toys to distract them. Moreover, their attention span will increase dramatically when they have fewer toys to play with, according to a study done at the University of Toledo.[2]

The typical American child is spoiled. They were born in an affluent country with a culture that over-consumes. Think about all the programs at Christmastime designed to make sure underprivileged kids get piles of toys, "just like our kids." We just can't stand to think that some kids out there aren't getting a pile of presents taller than the Christmas tree itself. In chapters 14 and 15, we're going to dive deeper into the perspectives we hold when it comes to giving.

The bottom line is, kids will become better at playing by themselves, and with others, if there are fewer things to play with and more to ignite their imaginations. We have become desensitized to the blessings all around us, whether that means a full playroom of toys or a well-stocked pantry. We still have trouble finding "anything to do," and "something to eat."

It's part of our culture to be discontent with what we have, and to always want more. That's what advertising feeds on. We can teach our kids to be content. And a great first step is fewer toys.

How Many Toys is Enough?

I think it's safe to say most American families could easily reduce the number of toys in their home by 50% and nobody would notice... yes, including your kids. In the rare event we've donated a toy one of our kids wanted to keep, they completely forgot about it within the same day we donated it. Our kids are typically fine with getting rid of lots of toys, because it creates lots of room for them to actually play.

There's no magic number on how many toys you need in

your home, but I think we can all admit we have too many. We can free up our children's space and time by eliminating some, if not most, of their toys.

Sit them down and explain how contentment and appreciation works before you start downsizing their toys. If they come home from school to a completely toy-free home, they're going to have some questions, and possibly some trust issues. It won't be easy to talk to them when they're upset about it.

Your kids may fight back on the idea of reducing their toys, so it's a good idea to do it gradually, but I promise they won't even remember they ever owned the toy once it's gone.

The Best Toys to Keep

How do you know which toys to keep, and which to get rid of? I suggest keeping the following types of toys, but you'll have to decide for yourself. This is what we kept:

- **Legos** – They spark creativity as kids build whatever they want, and they promote social play.
- **Board Games** – They teach many cognitive skills and promote social play. Though, some are more useful than others.
- **Crafts** – Often, anything that promotes creativity and art is worth keeping, especially when they can do the crafts with their siblings.
- **Educational Toys** – Things like a toy cash register to teach finance and math, or anything else that teaches a lesson.

Again, it comes down to intentional ownership. You can

keep as many toys in your home as you want, as long as you're intentional about why you keep what you keep. Every toy you keep doesn't have to be an educational tool—sometimes kids just need to play without thinking—but you are the one who gets to decide which toys you keep, and that's a big responsibility.

Keep the toys that will help, not hinder, your kids. Kids can make their own fun inside and outside without any toys at all. It's amazing the games kids come up with when their resources are limited.

## How to Get Rid of Your Toys

There are plenty of thrift stores and other places to donate your toys in the United States. Your church may be part of a mission that brings toys to kids around the world who literally don't have any. You could take your children's toy collection (or half of it) and spread it out across hundreds of kids who would be receiving their very first toy. Those kids would appreciate it and your children would be happier.

Let your kids see this in action. If your children have any doubts about getting rid of the toys, it will help to let them see how many other children they're helping by giving them the toys they didn't need in the first place.

Don't get so caught up on donating to the right cause that you keep the toys cluttering your house. Part of the reason you're doing this is to gain more space in your home and to own fewer things. Be responsible with how you give, but don't let that responsibility hold you back from giving.

If you can't find a great opportunity, just take it to any thrift store or church that's accepting donations. Or, with some of the low-quality toys out today, they may just need to go in the dumpster.

All of this talk about owning things leads directly to the reason we own so many things in the first place: consumerism. It can be a dangerous part of your children's lives. Advertising and marketing companies are devoted to making consumption the focus of our lives. That's what we're talking about next.

Summary – The Toy Trap

**Fewer Toys Leads to Happier Children**
The fewer toys children have, the more they appreciate the ones they do have.

It's part of our culture to be discontent with what we have and to always want more. That's what advertising promotes and feeds on. We can teach our kids to be content. And a great first step is fewer toys.

The best toys to keep:

- Legos
- Board games
- Crafts
- Educational toys

TWELVE

## AD ALERT

HOW ADVERTISING AFFECTS KIDS

"If you own this child at an early age... you can own this child for years to come."

MIKE SEARLES, PRESIDENT OF KIDS 'R' US

"It isn't enough to just advertise on television... You've got to reach kids throughout their day—in school, as they're shopping at the mall... or at the movies. You've got to become part of the fabric of their lives."

CAROL HERMAN, SENIOR VICE PRESIDENT OF GREY ADVERTISING

"Advertising causes conflicts at exactly the most vulnerable age for children to be in conflict with parents."

> JOHN C. CONDRY, DEPARTMENT OF HUMAN DEVELOPMENT, CORNELL UNIVERSITY

WHEN WAS THE LAST TIME ONE OF YOUR KIDS BEGGED, PLEADED, OR put on the cute expression you can't resist, in order to get you to buy them something at the store? Or maybe you have a teenager who likes to "educate" you on the coolest styles, trends, and brands. These are almost universal family rituals. And the pressure from the younger generation often works.

In fact, kids have the largest influence on family meals, entertainment choices, vacations, and many other aspects of life, according to a study on family lifestyles.[1] Advertisers know this and exploit it. Companies went from spending $100 million on advertising to kids in 1983, to spending over $17 billion on child-targeted advertising, annually, by 2007.[2]

Child-directed marketing is more prominent now than ever, and it's only getting worse. We can't change that, but we can help spread awareness.

Several studies reveal the alarming effects advertising has on our children. I've compiled the crucial facts and stats you need to know. Once you understand what's going on, you'll see how you can protect your kids.

## How Kids Influence Our Purchases

Why do marketing companies target kids? There are three primary reasons:

1. Kids are vulnerable and susceptible to advertisements.
2. Companies want to build brand loyalty from a young age.
3. Kids play a significant role in families' purchasing decisions.

Advertisers don't view all children equally. Marketing companies target children differently depending on the child's stage of life and what the company is trying to sell. This has caused advertisers to group kids into three different markets:

1. **Primary market** – Kids consuming with their own money
2. **Influence market** – Kids affecting parents' purchases
3. **Future market** – Kids' purchases once they're grown

The influence market goes deeper than you think. Marketing campaigns exploit children for something kids are known for: pestering their parents. Advertisers refer to this as "pester power."

From a marketing standpoint, this is a child's ability to nag until their parents buy things, whether for them or for the entire family. "We're relying on the kid to pester the mom to buy the product," says advertising executive Barbara Martino, "rather than going straight to the mom."

The pestering they're looking for comes in two forms:

1. **Persistence nagging** – A plea that is repeated by the children until the parents give in and make the purchase
2. **Importance nagging** – Guilting the parents into providing what's "best" for their kids (according to the marketing firm's definition of best)

Kids influence more purchases than we like to admit, and possibly more purchases than we even realize. Journalists Kim Campbell and Kent Davis-Packard explain, "The minivan was created, for example, because children demanded more room. Then they decided the three-door behemoth was uncool, helping give rise to the SUV."[3] And it doesn't end with family vehicles. James McNeal, a market researcher who specializes in the children's market, explains, "Every auto manufacturer has a strategy to target children."

Advertisers know how much your kids influence the vehicle you drive and other purchases you make. They use that to their advantage, and they continue from the influence market directly into the future market. Children are future customers and brand loyalty starts at a young age.

### Brand Loyalty in Children

Credit-Card Barbie carries a Visa, and it's not because the manufacturer wants Barbie to be lifelike; it's because Visa strategically endorses the product. Credit card companies know how heavily brand loyalty is tied to a young adult's first credit card. Over

70% of kids will keep their first credit card indefinitely.[4] This is a big deal for marketers. It's easy money—often for a lifetime.

Advertisers don't even wait until your children are old enough for their first Barbie. Babies can start forming mental images of logos they've seen, which leads to subconscious brand loyalty early on—as young as two years old, according to New Dream, an organization building awareness of children's overconsumption.

Two studies, dating back to 1944 and 1964, reveal that adults typically use 23% of the products they used when they were kids—mostly things used on a daily and habitual basis.[5] When a company gives away free products to a school (typically referred to as "sponsoring" the school or project), it's not just about the company "doing their part." Food companies such as Kraft, Pizza Hut, and Subway make their way into school lunchrooms with the idea of buying your children's brand loyalty. They make their branding highly visible for a reason.[6]

On average, children ages 2 to 11 see more than 25,000 advertisements a year on TV alone, not including product placement (when branded products are placed in an inconspicuous way to subconsciously market a product).[7] Advertisements are everywhere and your children pay much more attention to them than you do.

According to researchers with the American Psychological Association, "As children reach the age of 4 to 5 years, they typically perceive a categorical distinction between commercials and programming, but primarily on the basis of affective ('commercials are funnier') or perceptual ('commercials are shorter') cues only."[8]

Companies such as McDonalds and KFC market products

directly to children as "healthy options," when a complete study on advertising to children and nutritional value found few, if any, healthy choices at these restaurants.[9] No surprise there.

Some companies go a step further. Procter & Gamble actually has a panel of 250,000 teens who are asked to talk to their friends about P&G products.[10] This is a form of "buzz marketing" infiltrating our schools, and it's alarming. Yet advertising companies think this practice is perfectly fine. "I don't feel we're manipulating kids," says Kathy Lalley, senior vice president at Kid-Leo in Chicago, which handles accounts such as McDonalds and Nintendo. She believes they don't get kids to do anything they already wouldn't want to do. She goes on to say, "This society is a consumer society. Advertising, marketing and making brand decisions are part of life."[11]

It's obvious we can't rely on others to protect our kids from advertising. Schools and teachers don't. The marketers themselves clearly don't. This is another job left to the parents.

So, what can we do?

As with so many other things, intentional parenting charges in the side door to fight the good fight. It's our best defense mechanism.

### It's Not Just About the Ads

You can't shelter your kids from all forms of advertising, but you can be intentional about what your children are viewing. It's important to be intentional about what our children see, because once they've seen it, we can't take it back. Let's look at YouTube, for example.

I have no problems with YouTube as a whole. I've spent

some of the best, unexpected four-hour blocks of my life scrolling through their endless "related videos." However, you must know what you're subjecting your kids to, if you allow them free rein.

It's not just ads you have to worry about on YouTube. There have been some scary accounts of videos created specifically for children, but with highly inappropriate themes and images.

One popular example is the pseudo–Peppa Pig video, created by a random YouTuber, which depicts a graphic, violent scene at a dentist's office.[12] Though it looks like the real show upon first glance, and it was created for children to find, it's not something you would ever want them to find. It won't just ruin Peppa Pig for them; it could put disturbing images in their head that they can't get out.

It's simply too hard for YouTube, and other user-uploaded-video websites, to monitor everything. More than 400 hours of content are uploaded to YouTube every minute.[13] People who upload the videos know most parents aren't monitoring what their kids are watching. Don't be one of those parents. It's all related: advertising, marketing, unfiltered internet content. It's toxic. The only way we can fight toxicity is with intentionality.

As far as marketing goes, extended sessions on TV or YouTube will guarantee hundreds of ads in front of your kid's eyes, and possibly content worse than the ads. We've got to monitor what they're watching. This isn't just about "adult content," it's about indoctrination by all of these companies. We'll talk more about media and screen time in the next chapter.

## Protect Your Children From Marketing

Protecting our children starts with how we respond to these advertisements. For example, if we're giving in to impulse buys in the checkout line, how can we expect our kids to listen to us? We must control how we respond to marketing. It sounds redundant, but to model a proper response, we must first respond properly. We have to be real with ourselves about how advertising affects *us*.

The main way we can protect our kids is to teach them how advertising works. Teach your kids why they may want the toys, products, and food they think they want. Likewise, show your kids how marketers target you as well as them.

Show your children some examples of advertising, especially when it's right in front of you (I feel a teachable moment coming). When they see an ad, and want a product because of it, use that as a teachable moment to explain how marketing companies target them.

It's perfectly fine for your children to want toys or other things they see in advertisements. I'd be more concerned if they didn't. But it's important to help your children make their own decisions, without the help of some multi-billion-dollar advertising company. All these companies (and other influencers) are fighting for our attention. Our attention is like a currency that we need to be very deliberate with, because we have a limited supply. If our attention is always "consumed" by these "predators," we don't have the focus and attention we need for the things most important to us. We can choose where we want to put our attention, intentionally.

There are practical ways to protect your kids from advertisers and marketers. MediaSmarts[14] offers some helpful ideas for us to consider: [15]

- Have your children share product jingles, slogans, or ad campaigns they remember. Guide them to discuss why they think they remember these ads specifically and what makes them so powerful.
- Talk with your kids about why they think the internet is a powerful place for marketing, and how they are marketed to when they're on the web.
- Show your kids a TV program and have them explain the ads they remember throughout the show. Ask them why they think they remember those specifically.

If you're intentional and actively involved in your children's lives, you have the ability to combat all of the ads that will bombard them. Unmonitored media usage poses the biggest threat.

We must protect our children before the marketers get to them. If we raise marketing-conscious kids, we can fight the unwanted effects of marketing and advertising for future generations.

This leads us into one of the most important discussions in today's world: kids and technology.

Summary – Ad Alert

**How to Protect Your Children**
When it comes to intentional ownership, we have to protect our

children from certain things. The things they own, and the things they want, can be their downfall.

**Kids and Advertising**
Marketing companies target children for three reasons:

1. Kids are vulnerable and susceptible to advertisements.
2. Companies want to build brand loyalty from a young age.
3. Kids play a significant role in families' purchasing decisions.

Children are sorted into three categories by marketing companies:

1. **Primary market** – Kids consuming with their own money
2. **Influence market** – Kids affecting parents' purchases
3. **Future market** – Kids' purchases once they're grown

"Pester Power" comes in two forms:

1. **Persistence nagging** – A plea that is repeated by the children until the parents give in and make the purchase
2. **Importance nagging** – Guilting the parents into providing what's "best" for their kids (according to the marketing firm's definition of best)

Our children influence more purchases than we'd like to admit.

Babies are already starting to form mental images of company logos.

Companies target children because they want them to be consumers for life.

Be intentional about what your children are viewing and have conversations with them regularly about marketing and advertising.

THIRTEEN
# THE TECHNOLOGY THREAT
SMARTPHONES AND SCREEN TIME

"Children will watch anything, and when a broadcaster uses crime and violence and other shoddy devices to monopolize a child's attention, it's worse than taking candy from a baby. It is taking precious time from the process of growing up."

NEWTON N. MINOW, FEDERAL COMMUNICATIONS COMMISSION, 1961

"In this century, the mass media have come to rival parents, school, and religion as the most influential institution in children's lives."

*MEDIA AND VALUES MAGAZINE*

"We need desperately, I feel, a noncommercial alternative to what commercialism is trying to do to us. I'm not for censorship, but I'm certainly for self-censorship when it comes to producing or purveying products to America's children. I think that for people who make anything for children, their first thought should be: Would I want my child to see, hear, or touch this? And if the answer is no, just don't make it."

MISTER (FRED) ROGERS

---

My daughter had a heart-to-heart with me about getting a phone. She feels like she's missing out on a lot by not having a phone (namely, her friends' group chat). I told her I understood, but I think the risks outweigh the rewards right now (she's 13 years old and most of her friends have phones). We also had the fairly regular conversation about how we don't do things just because other people do them.

Then, we had the talk about how our family is different in many ways and I truly believe she will appreciate it when she gets older. When you live intentionally, you live differently. We also don't watch TV—other than the occasional family movie—so we're left out of conversations regarding the funniest new commercials or what point we're at in a TV series. The conversation with my daughter was interesting, but it gets even better in our household…

## Phones and Maturity Level

I was in the middle of writing this section when a situation came up with our oldest son. He brought home a phone he said was given to him. We later found out he actually saw it fall out of his classmate's pocket and he took it... he stole the phone. But wait... there's more!

When I went through the phone's contacts and found the kid's father, I sent a message to get the phone back to the original owner. That's when I figured out the child my son stole it from wasn't the original owner. The child had actually stolen this phone from someone else! I appreciate these kids giving me real-life scenarios, because I can't make this stuff up. The desire to fit in, and to have a handheld device, is *real*. This is why we need to stay so connected with our children. In our home, we constantly ask them about their day and everything going on in their life. We have regular and constant conversations.

These "funny" moments in life are learning points. What's the first thing my son did with this newly acquired phone? He searched for all the inappropriate content he could find on YouTube. Thankfully, it was mostly inappropriate music videos; it could've been much worse. I'm glad YouTube blocks *most* adult content.

We helped our son see why he isn't mature enough to own a smartphone yet and I really feel like it clicked. We also had a long conversation about stealing. He gave us the teachable moment. We're now awaiting a meeting with our son, the principal, and the two other students. It's going to be interesting.

Real conversations like this are what sparked the idea behind this section of the book. It brought up some important questions about children and phones. Are we limiting our kids socially by not allowing a phone until a later (than average) age? Possibly by a minuscule amount. By the way, the average age by which a child owns a smartphone today is around 10 years old.[1] On that note, should your kid have a smartphone, or a... [gasp] "regular" phone? Yes, they still have phones that only make phone calls. I will refer to those as "dumbphones" from here on, which is ironic, since they are so often the *smart* choice.

Owning a phone should depend on the need to have a phone, not on a specific age, or your child's self-proclaimed "need" to have a phone.

### Need-Based, Not Age-Based

Bill Gates says 14 is the "safest" age to give a child a cellphone.[2] While I actually love the fact that he advocates for a later age than most parents, I don't think it's something we should put a number on. If your child is 14, and walks home from school alone, or if they have a babysitting job that keeps them away from home at times, or if they have a part-time job working away from home... then sure, it's a good age for a cellphone. But if they're never left alone, and they're always in the care of an adult... do they *need* a phone? I don't think so. It's something for you to think about. You know, since it's your decision and all.

My friend's oldest [of six] son just started babysitting their younger children, at 12 years old. Now he has a phone, because it makes sense from a practical standpoint. What if an emergency comes up? He needs a phone. That being said, he does not have a smartphone. His phone is as dumb as the idea of a kid owning a phone just because they reach a certain age. Situations that warrant a cellphone shouldn't give full rights to a smartphone. The average U.S. consumer spends five hours a day on mobile devices.[3]

Not my children. What about yours?

There's a big difference between getting your child a phone to use during certain circumstances or a dumbphone for added safety and getting your child a smartphone with open internet access 24/7. Open internet access for teens (and younger) is happening more and more.

Here's how it goes. A child turns a certain age, or a need arises one time, and a smartphone comes to the rescue. You've seen it. Maybe you've done it. No judgment. But we have to think deeper into such an important issue. Given all the things a child can get into with an internet-accessible phone, I think it's worth taking the extra time to make an intentional decision.

If you don't think this is a serious issue, you may not be privy to some of the data out there. On a personal note, my friend's daughter recently tried to take her own life after being bullied on social media. Her daughter was fully connected to all kinds of social media networks and my friend didn't realize it was an issue until her daughter attempted suicide.

James P. Steyer, CEO of Common Sense Media, a nonprofit organization that reviews content and products for families, has a strict rule for his family: his children get a smartphone only when they start high school—after they have learned restraint and the value of face-to-face communication.[4] I think that's brilliant and it's intentional.

Along those lines, here are a few things to consider before getting your children a phone:

- Do they *need* a phone?
- Are they *responsible enough* to own a phone?

- Are they *pushing you* to get them a phone? If so, why?
- Can they *be trusted* with a phone when you're not there to monitor how they use it?
- Who is *paying for* the phone and the plan?
- If the phone has internet, *which content tracker/blocker* will you use?

A phone is a gateway to many great things, and many more not-so-great things. There's a lot of power in that small device. It's a big decision. Let's look at some more concerns…

Social Concerns & Risk Vs. Reward

As I said, my daughter wants a phone to chat with her friends. Am I limiting her socialization by not allowing her a phone? In some ways, yes. But after talking to her, I think it may have more to do with her friends' perception of her not having a phone. That's what she doesn't like, which is another issue altogether.

Don't get me wrong, a phone is a huge source of social interaction in today's world. I'm just not so sure it's a good medium to be using at 12 years old. People are constantly talking about how much teens are on their phones,[5] and once these teens hit their 20s, it doesn't change much. At least, not for the better. Nobody wants to have dinner with someone who can't put their phone down.

Technology is raising children in today's world. It's common to see a family at a restaurant, and the children's faces stuck in a phone, whether mom and dad's phone or their own. In fact, a popular reason to get kids their own phones is so the parents can bury their faces simultaneously. Smartphones destroy family conversations.[6]

When my daughter came to me with her concern of not having a phone, I assured her that her emotions are legitimate, and she isn't wrong for wanting to interact with her friends. When I pointed out the reasons I don't think she's ready for a phone, she had an even better understanding. We discussed some scary statistics from a recent study:

- 33% of parents and teens argue daily about device usage.
- 50% of children admit to being addicted to their devices.
- 72% of teens feel they must immediately respond to texts.
- 78% of teens check their devices at least hourly, often more.

We all know this is true. The same study[7] found 48% of parents feel the need to immediately respond to messages as well, so it's not just our children. We have to make sure we're setting the right example of healthy phone usage. Our kids are watching our actions more than they're hearing our words. It's not just about technology addiction. There is the "other" addiction you have to worry about when it comes to smartphones.

You probably know which addition I'm talking about.

## Smartphones and Pornography

Now for a brief interruption and a public service announcement.

I'm going to be blatant here and call it like it is. Are you ready for a *real* conversation?

Pornography is more easily accessible than ever, and it can ruin your child's life. Early exposure often leads to a lifelong addiction. Ninety-three percent of boys and 62% of girls are exposed to pornography in adolescence.[8] Pornography exposure at a young age can be devastating to a child's future sex life,[9] and it all too often stems from parents being too lazy to monitor their children's internet activity. Or simply too lazy to parent, letting the smartphone do it for them. I know I'm being harsh, but that's because this is serious. If you feel attacked, feel free to leave a bad review for this book, but it also may be a sign you need to look inward.

If your children are using the internet without any sort of monitoring, please wake up! There's a strong chance pornography has already entered their lives. Whether this is already an issue, or you're concerned with it becoming an issue, I highly recommend using accountability software. We personally use accountability software on all of our devices, to keep everyone accountable—myself included.

If you only take away one thing from this entire section, let it be about this point. Intentional parenting requires us, as the parents, to get involved in what our kids are doing. A teen living at home should get a certain amount of privacy, but not when it comes to electronic devices. It's not worth risking their future for their "privacy."

If you don't believe pornography is a true evil in the world, you may not know all the facts. On top of all the psychological effects, human trafficking is a real part of the internet pornography industry. When someone looks at porn, they're contributing to the industry. Aside from the fact that many of the actors in the movies are directly a part of human trafficking activity, the advertisements on pornography websites directly fund this kind of modern-day slavery more than you might think. It's worth doing some research to see the harmful effects of pornography and the direct relation it has to human trafficking.

So now that all the scary facts are out of the way, what is the right age? How do you know when it's time to get your kid a phone?

## What Age is the Right Age?

Again, I think children should get their own phone when they need one, not when they want one. We've been telling our children for a few years that they can have a phone if they come up with a good enough reason to own one. They have yet to do so, but they've tried.

Oh, have they tried.

Eventually there will be a good enough reason. But as it stands, they're never alone without access to an adult who has a phone, so they don't have that reason yet.

If you agree this should be a need-based decision, then you will know when it's the right time. But just for fun, let's go through each age group and see what the experts say.

Today's Parent released a great age-by-age guide on smartphones.[10] Here were the key findings:

- **Under 4** – No phone necessary.
- **Age 4 to 6** – A phone can be dangerous at this age. The brain is still developing and social skills can be impacted. Your child is much more likely to become

addicted to technology by having a phone at this age.
- **Age 7 to 9** – The experts say "no phones." Sure, you could argue this is old enough to have a phone, but the brain is still in a serious developmental stage, and all technology has a major impact at this age.
- **Age 10 to 12** – At this age, experts recommend the potential of kids owning a phone only to call their parents. It's still not the right age for a smartphone, or at least not one with internet access. A ScienceDaily study shows girls are particularly affected at this age, often negatively, by owning a smartphone.[11]
- **Over 12** – Teens should wait until they're 16 if at all possible. The later, the better. But 13 and on is a reasonable age to have a phone. It's still best to limit or eliminate internet access until they're at least 16.

While you may want to know the specific age to put on the decision, the above guidelines are as close as we can get. The main thing is to wait until it's absolutely necessary. It's easy to give into the "everybody's doing it" pressure and get your children a phone. So many kids have them before they're 12 and sometimes it's hard to know your kid is one of the few without one.

As I tell my kids, nobody ever looks back on the last year, or five or 10 years, and says, "I wish I would've spent more time watching TV and using my phone." Not having a phone won't ruin their life, but it just might save their future.

### Finding a Phone Solution

My entire goal behind this section is to leave you with a solution that's right for you. Since I can't possibly know your exact situation, here are some ideas.

**If you feel like your child isn't mature enough for a phone yet**, don't get them a phone. If there is no real need for a phone (i.e., your child doesn't go to any events alone), then there is no real reason for a phone.

**If you feel like your child does need a phone, but you don't trust them with a smartphone**, consider getting them a dumbphone. They still make plenty of basic flip-phones. Personally, I wouldn't trust any teen with a smartphone (I was a teen once, and I would not have trusted me with a smartphone—if smartphones were a thing when I was a teen). I know how prevalent inappropriate content is, and filtering services can be expensive, so a *dumb*phone seems like a *smart* solution.

**If you decide to get your kid a smartphone, or if they already have one**, it's difficult, but still possible to take it away after they have it. However, I understand if you don't want to do that. If you plan to let your kid keep the phone, here are some final guidelines I would suggest implementing:

- Make sure you have the password to the device.
- Let your child know you have the right to take it away at any point, if you see a reason.
- Set limits on the time your child can spend on their phone.
- Set the finance rules in stone, as far as who is paying for the phone and data, and what happens if the child uses additional data. Decide if they are only allowed

- Decide what will happen if the phone is broken or stolen, and who will pay for it.
- Specify off-limit times when your child is not allowed to use the phone.
- Explain you have the right to monitor everything your child is viewing, at any time, including text messages and social media.

These recommendations are based on what the Child Mind Institute suggests.[12] You have the overall say when it comes to your child having a phone. You make the call (no pun intended); your child doesn't.

Now we've got to address screen time in general. It's not just about having or not having a phone, it's also about how much time your child spends using the screen.

### The Media Threat and Screen Time

When I first got into non-fiction, I remember reading several self-help books and articles claiming to add time to your life… literally to every day of your life. How? In a roundabout way, they would tell you to stop watching TV.

It's true. Americans used to watch way too much TV. They still do, but media consumption has expanded. Hours spent in front of the TV have actually been on the decline. We are, however, spending hours in front of other types of media, and in most cases, we're wasting more hours than TV was stealing.[13]

There were a few years when people started to notice the decline in TV consumption, and thought we were doing better as a society. Over the last five years though, everyone is becoming aware of the fact that it's no better to mindlessly scroll Facebook or Snapchat than it is to mindlessly watch a series on TV (and with Netflix, binge-watching an entire series has become a new mode of media consumption). Actually, social media is all about instant gratification so it's worse for your mind than those Netflix sessions. At least we were finishing an entire episode when we were watching a TV series.

As parents, how are we to tackle mindless overconsumption of media? We combat mindlessness with intentionality... or more simply: mind*ful*ness. The first step is being mindful about everything that comes into our home, including media devices and the media itself. The latter is often not thoroughly considered.

How Much Screen Time?

I've talked to parents from every end of the screen-time spectrum. From parents who have no limit on their child's media consumption, to parents who don't allow any screen time at all. This is not one of those times where I will say there is no wrong answer, because I've seen the effects on kids without technology limits (and adults for that matter).

Sure, it's your decision. But if you're using media as a babysitter, you're doing it wrong (it being life). So, how much screen time should your kids be allowed?

First, remember *all* screen time counts: TV, phones, pads, computers, gaming devices, etc. Once you've decided it's the right time to give your child a phone, count that phone as screen time. If you don't want to follow your kids around all day to check their phone usage, you can find plenty of apps that do it for you. Older teenagers should be able to make their own decisions eventually, but early-teens and younger need a limit. For our kids, they'll have a limit as long as they live in our home. We limit ourselves, why wouldn't we limit our kids?

Once you get over one hour a day on technology, it starts getting dangerous. At that point, your children are going to start relying on, and needing, technology. One hour a day is a lot. I'm not saying you should give them that much. It's your call. But I would suggest—yes, as my own opinion—that one hour is the most you should consider for young children. If your kids don't get screen time every day (ours don't) then the hour cut-off isn't as vital. Here's what we do…

**Screen Time in Our Home**

We aren't anti-technology parents. Technology can be useful. Some apps and games are educational, but it's almost always low-quality education. It's good for a break here and there, but technology is not a teacher.

We allow our kids to play video games together on the occasional Saturday morning, because it actually helps them play well together. They can play for a few hours, because they likely won't be on technology the rest of the week. Screen time isn't a big deal in our home and our kids are fine with that. They don't even ask about more screen time.

Screen time is like candy, if your kids don't expect a lot each day, they won't have the craving for it. If they've grown up getting all they could possibly handle, it will be difficult (but possible) to break the habit. I use the candy analogy, because we have some friends who raised their son without ever giving him a piece of candy, and now, at five years old, he doesn't like candy when he tries it. I'm not saying that directly correlates to screen time, but if you think about it, it's a pretty good analogy. Seriously, think about it.

If our kids need to use the computer, all they have to do is ask, but they are monitored closely when they have internet access. It's easy to overlook how dangerous media can be. We blow it off and insist "everyone" lets their kids do it. We should be more intentional than "everyone." It's our job to protect our children from the world when they're too young to understand what they need protection from. We just discussed what they need protection from. The threat is real.

Summary – The Technology Threat

**Dealing With Kids and Phones**
Phones should be need-based, not age-based.

Ask these questions before getting a phone for your children:

- Do they *need* a phone?
- Are they *responsible enough* to own a phone?
- Are they *pushing you* to get them a phone? If so, why?
- Can they *be trusted* with a phone when you're not there to monitor how they use it?
- Who is *paying for* the phone and the plan?
- If the phone has internet, *which content tracker/blocker* will you use?

The social benefits of owning a smartphone don't outweigh the risks. Consider a dumbphone.

When/if you decide to get your children a smartphone, take proper precautions by having full access to it, and consider getting accountability software.

**The Media Threat and Screen Time**
Screen time should be limited in one form or another, but it's up to you to set the limit.

Once screen time crosses the hour-a-day line, children start to become dependent on it.

## FOURTEEN
# GROWING GRATITUDE
#### RAISE GRATEFUL GIVERS IN AN ENTITLED WORLD

"Cultivate the habit of being grateful for every good thing that comes to you, and to give thanks continuously. And because all things have contributed to your advancement, you should include all things in your gratitude."

RALPH WALDO EMERSON, FAMOUS ESSAYIST,<br>PHILOSOPHER, AND POET

"In ordinary life, we hardly realize that we receive a great deal more than we give, and that it is only with gratitude that life becomes rich."

DIETRICH BONHOEFFER, FROM *LETTERS AND*<br>*PAPERS FROM PRISON*

"Gratitude turns what we have into enough."

ANONYMOUS

---

> "And he sat down opposite the treasury and watched the people putting money into the offering box. Many rich people put in large sums. And a poor widow came and put in two small copper coins, which make a penny. And he called his disciples to him and said to them, 'Truly, I say to you, this poor widow has put in more than all those who are contributing to the offering box. For they all contributed out of their abundance, but she out of her poverty has put in everything she had, all she had to live on.'"

MARK 12:41-44

This is the story of "The Widow's Offering." If you grew up in church, you've probably heard it before. I was in my mid-20s the first time I heard it. It's a beautiful story about how a woman gave less than everyone else in a monetary sense, but more than everyone else because she gave all she had. Giving comes from gratitude. It's hard to give from your heart if you're not grateful. Giving shouldn't be forced. Furthermore, giving shouldn't be *forced on* your kids. It should be something they want to do and you have a hand in helping them want to do it.

You can extinguish entitlement in your kids and introduce

gratitude. Remembering to be thankful is difficult for adults, and it won't come naturally to children. It's easy to get caught up in our daily routines and forget to take a moment to be grateful for all of our blessings. When we're rushing around in our busy lives, we can become complacent. We rush from school to football practice to grab a quick dinner, without stopping to be grateful for the teachers, coaches, and cooks.

We all do it. And we could all use help in the area of gratitude. Have you noticed studies and research are all starting to show gratitude is one of the biggest, if not *the* biggest, factor in long-term happiness?[1] Counting your blessings is actually one of the first methods used to treat or prevent depression. It's also one of the first strategies in military suicide prevention training. Because it's effective.

I've compiled some ideas to help teach our children this before they start to take things for granted. We will always need to be reminded to be thankful, but the younger the idea is instilled, the more natural gratitude becomes.

Start Small

Gratitude doesn't mean taking an hour out of your day to name a million things you're grateful for; it just means remembering to say thanks for everything you have. And while you're not going to remember everything you have, you have to start with something.

**The Dinner-Table Habit**

Our family adopted a habit before dinner every night. We

each say one thing we're thankful for before we eat. This isn't a time to criticize the things children are grateful for; it's a time to teach your kids to be thankful for the different things in their life. If they say they're thankful for their mom and dad, encourage them and reinforce how nice it is that they appreciate you. If they say they're thankful for candy, be thankful they're thankful for something.

You can use this method upon waking up each day, before bed, right after school, or almost anywhere else, because it's so quick. You don't want to bombard your children with saying thanks a thousand times a day. Start small and add some gratitude moments slowly. Your kids will actually enjoy this from the start, if it doesn't feel like a chore. Nowadays, if we ever forget to do the dinner-table habit before we eat, we're quickly reminded by one, if not all five, of our children.

Practice Gratitude

Your children see what you do before they hear what you say.

If you're not grateful, your children aren't going to be grateful. A recent study showed how our level of gratitude is one of the most important factors in our children's level of gratitude.[2] They're simply proving what we all know to be true in our hearts: actions speak louder than words.

It's ironic that another study showed how parents are frustrated when their kids don't express gratitude,[3] yet we so often go through our days complaining and being ungrateful.

You must model the gratitude habit. When your kids hear your language of gratitude, they're more likely to imitate it. Even if they seem annoyed by how much you express gratitude, the habit will rub off. Watch what you're doing before you look too closely at what your kids are doing.

## Model Contentment

There's a big difference between complacency and contentment. Contentment is being able to appreciate where you are and what you have. Complacency is taking contentment too far and getting stuck. This is another area we must model for our children.

If you're constantly talking about wanting a nicer house, car, job, or anything of the sort, then your kids are going to learn that happiness and contentment is always one more thing or situation away from where you are right now. In *The Illusion of Money: Why Chasing Money is Stopping You from Receiving It*, Kyle Cease talks about contentment, and how it always seems to be one step away. He put it brilliantly when he said, "The more abundance I had, the more lack I could find."

Teach your children how to be happy right now, with what they have. This is such an important lesson for us to learn too, so make it easy on your kids by teaching it at a young age. The materialistic chasing of the next great thing is killing gratitude across the country.

## Teach the Importance of Relationship

> "And let the peace of Christ rule in your hearts, to which indeed you were called in one body. And be thankful."

COLOSSIANS 3:15

Gratitude is a huge part of Paul's teaching in the New Testament and you'll find the same in the teachings of Jesus. Gratitude is often reflected in our relationships and thankfulness is often taught alongside relationship. Studies show, relationships and gratitude are connected.[4]

Whether it's a relationship with God or people, social interaction with like-minded individuals is good for gratitude. We can teach our kids this by modeling what relationships should look like within our family and with close friends.

Materialism kills gratitude and relationship kills materialism. When your kids value people more than the acquisition of stuff, not only will they be happier, but they will experience more gratitude.

Here's one thing that's sure to help them appreciate what they have...

Show Your Kids True Poverty

You're going to seriously annoy your kids by constantly saying things like, "you should be thankful for your food; there are kids in Africa who haven't eaten in days," and it's not going to teach them to be grateful. It's going to teach them to be annoyed at the very children you're trying to make them feel sympathy for. That being said, if you show them what poverty really looks like, they may just start listening when you compare their life to other kids' lives who actually have it rough.

Mission trips are great for this, but you don't have to look far to find poverty. In fact, the farther away you travel, the more disconnected your children will feel from the people you're helping. Your town, or the closest major city, is far enough to find a place to help. Drive around and show your children how good they really have it. Teach the importance of caring for the poor and the homeless. It's not about feeling sorry for people who are worse off, it's simply caring about people in general. An "us and them" mindset isn't what you're going for.

The ultimate goal is empathy, not sympathy.

You *don't* want your kids to feel guilty for the life they have, but you *do* want them to feel empathy for those who aren't doing so well. Your children will likely feel so much sympathy that they will want to help, which leads to true empathy. That, of course, starts with their heart...

### Instill a Giving Heart

If you can instill the desire to give in your child's heart, half the battle is already won. God loves a cheerful giver. Giving blesses the giver as much as the receiver. When your children start to become focused on others, not just on themselves, gratitude will follow. There are several practical ways to teach your children to be cheerful givers:

- **Involve your children in your giving.** Show them how you give, whether to church or charity, and explain how happy it makes you. Show them *you* are a cheerful giver.
- **Take it easy on their giving.** While it's important to teach your children to give, don't force it. State your case for why they should give and let them make the final decision.

- **Give in more ways than one.** Your child may love giving their time, but may be a little reluctant to give money. Or vice versa. Teach them to be open to other forms of giving by focusing on what they enjoy. Don't force a specific style of giving, cultivate the form they enjoy, and it will branch out from there.
- **Go where they can see their giving.** Volunteer at a soup kitchen or a homeless shelter and take your kids along. They may just fall in love with giving and serving others.

If you model gratitude and thankfulness, your children will follow in your footsteps. Many children are far from cheerful givers. In fact, it's becoming more common to see almost the exact opposite, which manifests itself in the form of entitlement.

Let's talk about entitlement...

### The Entitlement Mentality

There are actual studies showing kids today are 25% more entitled than older generations and 50% more entitled than the oldest generation.[5] But I don't think we need studies to see how the entitlement mentality is taking its course. Plus, I'll admit, entitlement seems like a weird thing to quantify into statistics, but as it translates into behaviors, we can all see it's a problem.

This isn't a political topic. This is not a "fix our youth" topic. I don't want to lay blame. I'm simply trying to shine light on an issue we all face with our kids. Let's see how we can deal with this, for their sake.

### What is Entitlement Mentality?

A basic definition from the Cambridge Dictionary defines entitlement as, "the feeling that you have the right to do or have what you want without having to work for it or deserve it, just because of who you are." Therefore, entitlement mentality happens when entitlement becomes second nature, or an assumed "fact."

So what's the opposite of entitlement? One informal opposite —the first term that comes to my mind—is adversity. It's not a literal opposite. It's the opposite insofar as kids who experience adversity tend to refuse an entitlement mentality.

Entitlement instills the idea that you don't have to work for things, yet they should still be given to you, because you are… you. Adversity takes from you when you have nothing left to give, which is why kids raised in an adverse environment often grow up to be the happiest and most successful. That's why the poorest countries are often the happiest. It all comes back to appreciating what you have, which is actually easier to do when you have less.

We shouldn't force adversity on our kids, but we can learn from adversity's effects and use that to help raise our kids, without always giving them the easy way out. It's easy to see how an entitled mindset can be dangerous and mostly how it can be devastating for a child's future. Entitlement goes against reality, because in life, you can't expect to be given things just because you are you.

**Note:** I'm not going to get into entitlement in regards to racial injustice. While that's a crucial topic and currently front and center in the news, it's a topic for a different book. An important book, but not this book.

## Excuses and Entitlement

Excuses go along with the entitlement mentality. "I don't have to do this because someone else will do it," or "you *have* to do this because I *want* you to do this." Any excuses our children use should be discussed and hopefully diminished completely, especially if the excuse stems from entitlement.

Excuses are never helpful, even if they're justified. For example, the family who is in tremendous debt, due to unexpected medical bills, won't solve their problem by explaining *why* they're in debt. We must react to our circumstances in a healthy way. We can't control our circumstances. We can control our response.

There are legitimate excuses. But they still don't help, and holding on to excuses can lead to entitlement and inaction. Regardless of how "legit" the excuse is, the excuse itself helps no one involved.

## How to Fight Entitlement in Our Kids

So, what can we do to prevent our kids from growing up with an entitled mindset? Replace entitlement with gratitude. We have to fight the fictitious idea that things are given to us for no reason at all.

Entitlement breeds the "I'll be happy when…" mindset we talked about earlier. Why wait to be happy? Yet, we're almost all guilty of it.

"I'll be happy *when* I get that promotion."

"I'll be happy *when* we move to a bigger city."

"I'll be happy *when* I get married… or divorced… or married to someone else."

Entitlement is a lie that says you deserve more, but gratitude and contentment can overcome that lie. Contentment is appreciating where you are in life and being grateful for all the things you have throughout your journey. You can strive for more, while also appreciating where you are.

Don't feel guilty for what you *can't* give your kids; teach them contentment and gratitude for what you *can* give them. Children can thrive on a love for God and a love for others. The things this world offers pale in comparison.

If you feel like your kids may be entitled (which most of our kids probably are… at least a little), start working on gratitude, contentment, and giving. It's the fastest way for your kids to learn what truly matters.

This leads us right into the most common way we all *give* in our lives: through gifts for others. I want to offer a new perspective on gift giving, in light of the minimalist mindset, and as a content Christian.

## Summary – Growing Gratitude

**How to Instill Giving and Gratitude in Your Children**
Gratitude doesn't mean taking an hour out of your day to name a million things you're grateful for; it just means remembering to be thankful for everything you have. Try the dinner-table habit.

**Practice Gratitude**
If you want to raise grateful children, you must practice gratitude.

A lack of gratitude comes from a lack of contentment. Teach your children how to be happy right now, with what they have.

### The Importance of Relationship
Whether it's a relationship with God or people, social interaction with like-minded individuals is good for gratitude.

We can teach our kids this by modeling what relationships should look like within our family and with close friends.

### Show Your Kids True Poverty
The ultimate goal is empathy, not sympathy.

You *don't* want your kids to feel guilty for the life they have, but you *do* want them to feel empathy for those who aren't doing so well.

### Instill a Giving Heart
There are several practical ways to help your children be givers:

- Involve your children in your giving.
- Nurture their giving but don't force it.
- Give in more ways than one.
- Go where they can see the impact of their giving.

### The Entitlement Mentality
Entitlement instills the idea that you don't have to work for things, yet they should still be given to you, because you are you.

Children are more entitled today than ever, according to studies.

Entitlement is often accompanied by excuses, but excuses help no one.

**How to Fight Entitlement in Our Kids**

Fight entitlement with gratitude.

Entitlement mentality tells you that you deserve more. Gratitude and contentment will overcome entitlement.

FIFTEEN
## RETHINKING PRESENTS
A NEW PERSPECTIVE ON GIFT GIVING

"Because only in America, people trample others for sales exactly one day after being thankful for what they already have."

ANONYMOUS

"Can it really be my duty to buy and receive masses of junk every winter?"

C. S. LEWIS, FROM *GOD IN THE DOCK*

"Are these things really better than the things I already have? Or am I just trained to be dissatisfied with what I have now?"

CHUCK PALAHNIUK, FROM THE NOVEL, *LULLABY*

> "Probably the reason we all go so haywire at Christmas time with the endless, unrestrained and often silly buying of gifts is that we don't quite know how to put our love into words."
>
> HARLAN MILLER, AUTHOR

---

In the 1905 short story, "The Gift of the Magi," by O. Henry, Della Young goes Christmas shopping on Christmas Eve to find a present for her husband, Jim. But she didn't have any money. So, she decided to sell her hair for $20 to a local hairdresser so she could buy her husband's gift.

Della sees a platinum pocket watch chain—the perfect gift, she thinks. She buys the chain and goes home to give the gift to Jim. When she gets home, they exchange gifts. Jim goes first and gives her a nice set of combs for her beautiful long hair, which he can see she no longer has. Della admits she sold her hair to fund his gift. When she gives the chain to Jim, he admits he sold his pocket watch to fund the set of combs. They're both left with some useless new possessions, but with a greater gift of knowing they each loved each other enough to sell something precious for the other's gift.

This isn't the typical Christmas story. It's almost a Romeo and Juliet type of plot twist, but it was an important Christmas to each of them, because the gifts expressed a true sense of love for one another. Of course, this isn't how gift giving typically goes in today's world. Christmas gifts often turn away from the true "reason for the season" and move into the realm of greed and consumerism. A quick internet search will show you the war going on between the anti-consumerists who say Christmas is *all about* consumerism and the advocates who say Christmas *isn't about* consumerism. There's a middle ground. We all know there is a consumeristic aspect to Christmas in the minds of many and we would likely agree that we don't want our kids to think of Christmas as a time focused purely on receiving presents. We've already looked at consumerism, but we haven't looked at how it affects gift giving. Parents expect to spend close to $1,000 on Christmas gifts for their children each year,[1] and somehow the average shopper manages to rack up even more than that in holiday debt.[2]

As a society, we're teaching our children they deserve a big Christmas and that presents come before financial responsibility, while neither of those things are true. In American culture, our kids put a lot of emphasis on presents, because *we* put a lot of emphasis on presents. But there's a better way to think about gift giving, receiving presents, and material entitlements. I'm going to show you a different [and slightly controversial] side to such a commonly held belief.

This is an area my wife and I have struggled with for years. Namely, teaching our children gratitude, while not giving them so much that it causes a sense of entitlement. I'm going to lay out what we've tried, what we've learned, and what we're still learning.

## Fighting Consumerism in Kids

We try hard to make sure our kids aren't engulfed in consumerism. It's not easy, so it requires us being intentional in every shopping experience. While we don't always succeed, this is how we try to frame shopping...

Our young kids aren't allowed to ask for anything in stores.

It got out of control. They were asking for everything. Things they wanted and things they didn't even care about, but just "needed" to have. So we cut them off. Our children are free to have open discussions about things they may get later on—as a present or by saving their own money—but they will not be leaving the store with something we didn't intend to buy before we walked in. Once they're old enough to make their own spending decisions, we walk them through the process. We don't stop our older kids from making purchases, but we let them know when they're making impulse buys.

We try to carry this idea over into gift giving. We don't want our kids to grow up expecting presents for every occasion and connecting material possessions to the holiday season. We still give gifts in our home, but we have dumped the traditional idea of gift giving.

### Dump Traditional Gift Giving

The average American child receives 70 new toys per year.[3] Seventy? We may be going a bit overboard as a country. Whether it's a birthday, Christmas, or other occasion, consider four reasons why traditional gifts aren't worth it:

1. It takes a lot of money to buy gifts for people who likely don't need anything else to clutter their home and life.
2. It takes a lot of time to shop for gifts—time that could be spent with each other making memories instead of amassing material possessions.
3. I've never heard anyone say, "I don't think we have

enough stuff in our house,"—I know I've never said that.
4. We often get things we didn't really want as gifts and keep them out of obligation—sometimes for years.

There are other ways to give, rather than the traditional mountains of presents on the birthday table, or under the Christmas tree.

We're going to look at both occasions.

**Birthday Parties**

Our family doesn't do typical birthday parties. At this point, I'm sure that doesn't surprise you. We've done them in the past and finally decided they weren't for us. In our conversations with other parents, we've noticed they do birthday parties because they think they're "supposed to," or because they grew up doing them. It's good to question things we've "always done," but admittedly, we don't always think to question something we've always assumed was a normal part of life.

Growing up, I had a few birthday parties on the "big ages," like 16, 18, and 21, but other than that, I didn't really have parties per se. We've taken a similar approach with our kids, and here's how it works:

- **Birthday dinners, not parties** – Instead of a birthday party, our kids get to pick where they want to go out to dinner, and they can invite a few friends.
- **Experiences, not things** – Instead of physical gifts, we prefer to give experiences, like trips and anything else

that brings our family together and doesn't clutter our home.
- **Time, not gifts** – We make it clear their friends don't need to bring gifts (we actually prefer people don't bring gifts, because it puts the focus on stuff instead of the time together).
- **Immaterial, not material** – If their friends absolutely have to bring a gift, we prefer digital or monetary gifts.

The grandparents typically put some money in the children's college funds and they'll give them some spending money as well. That's what we do, but that may not work for you. There are all kinds of ways to dump traditional birthday parties for more intentional ones. Fiver parties are another popular alternative to traditional birthday parties.

**Fiver Parties**

I wanted to briefly touch on the new trend of fiver parties. I'll leave you with this as a final idea on birthday parties, but the point is, know why you're doing birthday parties the way you do them.

Lana Hallowes from Babyology[4] explains fiver parties:

*"In short, a fiver party is an end to all of our kid present-buying woes! It is simply a birthday party where all the little guests bring a $5 note to go towards a big ticket present that the parents have bought and which the child really wants."*

I think it's a great idea for reducing clutter, and it makes more sense, financially, for everyone involved. You don't end up with a bunch of small toys your children don't need, and a few days (hours? minutes?) later, don't really want.

As parents, we're not obligated to get our children any physical gifts. If you like the idea of gifts at birthday parties, fiver parties could work for you. Now let's talk about where the big bucks are spent: Christmas gifts.

**Rethinking Christmas Gifts**

I love Christmas. It's my favorite time of the year, but I stress a little too much over the new clutter expected each year. I know it's coming. Or, at least, it will *try* to make its way into our home.

We would all agree Christmastime is more about spending time together than receiving presents. Of course, marketing companies would convince us otherwise. And we may say we feel like time together is more important, while our [and our children's] actions show we think the opposite.

Joshua Becker[5] gives some great insight on how gift giving has gotten out of control:

- 28% of shoppers are entering the holiday season still paying off debt from last year's gift shopping![6]
- Over 50% of holiday shoppers either overspend their holiday budget or do not set one at all.[7]
- Consumers who went into debt over the holiday season racked up an average of $1,054 in new debt over the timeframe.[8]

Then Joshua shows how these gifts aren't helping anything, they're only making matters worse, because:

- 53.1% of people report receiving unwanted gifts during Christmas.[9]
- $16 billion is wasted on unwanted gifts every year.[10]
- Some reports indicate up to 18% of gifts are never used by the person who receives them. Four percent are immediately thrown into the trash.[11]
- Whenever I speak on minimalism and take questions afterward, the two most common questions are 1) How do I implement minimalism in a family? And 2) How do I handle and/or tell loved ones to stop giving me so many gifts?

Gift giving feels like a loving act, and it may come from the heart, but it's causing problems. For a consumeristic society, gift giving is almost harmful. We all know we have turned Christmas into a time of receiving and strayed from the true meaning. I've heard it said, "let's take Christmas back for compassion, not consumption." I think that's a pretty good idea.

Many celebrities are starting to advocate the idea of giving few to no gifts to their children at Christmastime. I'm not saying I agree with all the reasons celebrities are doing it. I'm also not saying being a celebrity makes you an authority on anything outside of your specialty, but one couple did stand out to me.

Chip and Joanna Gaines, HGTV stars, said they have their kids pick out presents to give to children in struggling families,[12] where the presents likely mean a lot more. I love that, and I think this habit would benefit all of our children more than receiving a mountain of presents ever would.

## Give Presence, Not Presents

I couldn't resist that heading… but seriously, giving the gift of being there is more important to your kids than material presents, whether they realize it or not in the moment. How do you "give" presence? Here are a few options:

- **Vacation** – Instead of spending hundreds of dollars on presents for your children, consider taking them on a family vacation. It gets you away from work to spend time with your family and you'll make some of the best memories. If you don't take an annual vacation, the money you've been spending on presents may just be the funding you've been looking for.
- **Daddy/Mommy Dates** – We like to do these regularly. If you don't do these at all, they're an amazing opportunity to connect with your kids individually, especially if you have several children. If you do these on a normal basis, consider having special, full days together with each one of your children. This may require you to take a day off work; you may need it.
- **Volunteer** – This could be the most life-changing thing on here. Around Christmastime especially, if you go with your kids to volunteer at a homeless shelter, soup kitchen, or elsewhere, they will get to spend time with you, and give to others. It's important to branch out on this one. If you serve at your local church all the time, consider finding a new outlet for this special occasion.

We always prefer to give experiences instead of products.

"Presence over presents" seems to be a majority opinion, actually. Sixty-nine percent of Americans said they would skip exchanging gifts during the holidays if their friends and family agreed to it, according to a survey conducted by Harris Poll, on behalf of SunTrust Banks, Inc.[13]

If you still decide to give physical presents, consider the long-term cost (read: clutter) of the things you buy. Is it worth making little Bobby happy, for a few minutes in front of the Christmas tree, just to deal with all the clutter for years to come? There's a good chance Bobby won't even remember he has most of that stuff by next year, but you'll still be staring at it for a while.

**Grandparents:** *If you're running into issues with grandparents buying your kids way too much stuff, have a conversation with them. Show them some of the ideas to give non-material gifts. This is a common issue, but it's fixable with a simple conversation. If you are a grandparent, take these things into consideration for your adult children's sake.*

To Give or Not to Give?

After all of this, that is still the question. People value gifts they're given 20% less than they value items they buy for themselves, according to economist, Joel Waldfogel.[14] Joel took an economic look at the subject, and he explains why gift giving—especially careless gift giving—is much less necessary than we think. It's actually harmful in a lot of ways. Consider this excerpt from his article:

"It's bad enough that we buy a lot of stuff that no one wants. It turns *out we buy it using money we don't yet have. It wasn't always this way. In the 1930s, almost 10 percent of Christmas spending was financed with money squirreled away into Christmas clubs—bank accounts paying little interest but helping consumers save for the holiday. Participants promised to contribute weekly, frequently as little as $0.25 at a time. These accounts were popular because they helped even unsophisticated consumers—many of whom didn't have another bank account—avoid the temptation to fritter their money away. Since 1970, by contrast, the explosive growth in consumer credit has had the opposite effect, helping consumers fall prey to their lack of self-control when it comes to borrowing. In recent years, one-third of holiday spending is still not paid off two months after Christmas."*

Even if you're a phenomenal gift giver, there's still a chance someone won't like the gift, and they'll feel obligated to keep it, which leads to a cluttered home. Think about the clutter in your home. How much of the random stuff is there because someone special bought it for you and you *just can't* give it away?

Consider *giving* outside your home to those who really are in need, instead of *getting* inside your home where you already have too much stuff. Get your kids on board. Giving to a cause is better than giving to each other in so many ways. We already have so much. As with everything else, it comes back to being intentional.

Intentional parenting. Intentional giving. Intentional living. If you're intentional in all you do, all you do will be blessed. Giving, in itself, obviously isn't the problem, because giving is a beautiful thing. But we need to replace mindless giving with intentionality. Here's a great example of what I mean…

Joan Lunden, former co-host of ABC's, Good Morning America, says, "We give promissory notes for kindnesses we're happy to provide." She goes on to explain how others could do the same: "Bosses could bring in a fitness instructor or massage therapist to the office... the gift of health to their employees."[15] It's intentional, thoughtful, and it doesn't involve buying more stuff. The same school of thought can be applied to any business or home.

Immaterial Gift Ideas

I want to leave you with some ideas for giving without buying physical things. We already talked about some of these above, but this is a more exhaustive list. Whether you're buying for family or friends, here are some great immaterial gift ideas[16] to buy for others (and great things to ask for):

- Vouchers for things like massages, car washes, house cleaning, landscaping... anything you could think of that would help someone out for a day. The voucher could be from a company, or a homemade voucher for you to perform the service.
- Plan a day trip together. Your children, parents, other family, or friends would really appreciate this. It could be a day hike, kayaking trip, visit to a new city, or anything else you think up.
- Consumables like baked goods, fruit baskets, flowers, candy or anything that won't be in the home for long.
- Volunteer as a family, or group of friends, at a local homeless shelter, soup kitchen, or any unique volunteer opportunities in your town.

- Buy a gym membership or personal trainer for a certain time period.
- Create an online scrapbook. There are too many services to list, but find one that works for you. Upload your family photos and share them with your family and friends. Allow them to upload photos too, and it becomes a gift for everyone.
- Ask people to donate to your favorite charity, or to your local church, instead of buying you something. Do this for others as well. It just takes a little prodding to figure out where your family and friends would love to see money applied. Try to figure it out inconspicuously so it's a big surprise.
- Buy a subscription like Audible or Spotify for however long you see fit. If they're already subscribed, pay for a set amount of time.

You can take those ideas and stretch them into hundreds of options. We'd all be better off if we gave more time and fewer things.

Unfortunately, the reason kids receive so many gifts is often because the entire home is centered around the children. I understand this, because it's natural to want to give your children everything you can, but a child-centered home is not only dangerous... it's our next topic.

Summary – Rethinking Presents

**A New Perspective on Gift Giving**
We can raise children to give differently and intentionally.

Dump the idea of traditional gift giving.

Think before you give. Be intentional about how and why you give gifts.

Consider these options for your children instead of traditional giving:

- Take a family vacation.
- Go on a daddy/mommy date.
- Volunteer with your children.

There are many immaterial gifts you can give to your children and others.

## SIXTEEN
# GOD-CENTERED HOME
### THE DANGERS OF A CHILD-CENTERED HOME

"But seek first the kingdom of God and his righteousness, and all these things will be added to you."

MATTHEW 6:33

"Jesus Christ is the same yesterday and today and forever."

HEBREWS 13:8

"The Scriptures can become a powerful source of protection as we invite God and his words to stand guard over our homes."

EMILY BELLE FREEMAN, FROM *CREATING A CHRIST-CENTERED HOME*

You've seen the social media posts and memes:

"My child is the most important thing in the universe to me."

"There's nothing more important than my children."

"My children are my life."

Those are all phrases uttered with the best intentions and the utmost love, but these ideas are contrary to how a healthy home functions.

In a child-centered home, the entire household revolves around the children. Everything you do, eat, play, attend, plan for, and prepare for... revolves around the kids. But you love your children with every ounce of your soul, so what's so bad about this? Well, I'll tell you, because I've witnessed it, and I continue to witness it. It creates disaster.

You may not completely realize your kids are your entire life. At least, not yet. Because one day, they're going to move out. Then what? Well, then you'll realize you weren't their entire life. That can be a dangerous spot to be in. A spot that could lead to depression and a lack of fulfillment in anything else you do.

I'm glad you're still reading, regardless of whether you're intrigued or fuming. Before we go on, here are six reasons why a child-centered home is bad for you and your kids:

1. **It's not a child-centered world.** The world isn't centered on any single person. Of course, if the world was centered on Jesus, we wouldn't have many of the issues we face today, but we all know it's not, and it's definitely not centered on your child.
2. **Your children will grow up thinking it's all about them.** When they leave home and see it's not all about them, they could become depressed, or at minimum, confused. They grew up as the center of your world,

and now they're out in the world, and they may not be the center of anything.
3. **Kids are automatically selfish.** Don't make it worse. We spend so many of their younger years teaching our kids not to be selfish. Humans are selfish by default, so selflessness is something that must be learned. It's not easy to embrace selflessness, but once your kids do, they'll be happier.
4. **You don't take care of yourself.** When you think life is all about your kids, you make sacrifices. Those sacrifices are great when they're healthy. It's a problem when you sacrifice all the time for your kids, and end up abusing yourself, because you've kept the "it's all about them" mindset for so long. If you don't take care of you, you can't do a good job of taking care of others.
5. **It's a burden on your marriage.** When you put anything before God, and anything other than God ahead of your spouse, you're taking things out of God's designed order. What happens when your kids move out and leave you with an empty nest? You may realize you barely know your spouse anymore if you've put your kids first for 20 years.
6. **It puts your kids in charge.** Whether you realize it or not, in a child-centered home, your kids are in charge. The problem is, they aren't ready for that kind of responsibility. They shouldn't have to absorb the responsibility of always getting their way (that's the definition of entitlement that we discussed earlier). It's only going to hurt them. I know it's initially easier to give in, and it's tough to say "no" and let them learn

difficult lessons by messing up without your help, but it will make their adult life so much easier if they aren't in charge when they're younger.

So, if you agree a child-centered home isn't the best option, and that you can love your kids with all your heart without having a child-centered home, let's look at how to avoid a home controlled by your kids' wants and needs…

How to Avoid a Child-Centered Home

What's better than a child-centered home? What do you turn to instead? A God-centered home. Center yourself and your family on your faith. We center ourselves and our family on Jesus and everything makes more sense when we do. I'm not saying it's easier, but it's better.

You're going to be with your kids for at least 18 years and then they'll be living on their own. You'll be with your spouse for the rest of your life, but you'll be with Jesus for the rest of eternity. So it makes sense, logically, to put Jesus first, and then your spouse, and then your kids.

I'm not going into the ethical dilemma of "what if there's a fire, and your wife and kids are in the house, and you can only save one…" No, that's not what I'm talking about here. I'm talking about the basic order of life.

When you focus on Jesus, and keep a strong marriage, you're going to love your kids, and they're going to know it. The best thing you can do for your kids is to have a strong marriage and model a Christ-like life for them.

Love your children, but don't idolize your children. Be careful with phrases like, "my kids are more important than anything else." Healthier phrases are, "I love my kids with all my heart" or, "I'm raising Godly kids who love the Lord."

## What About Single-Parent Homes?

I didn't forget about all the single mothers and fathers out there. The ones who are sacrificing daily to provide a great life for their kids. You guys are doing great. I'm not saying you should love your kids any less, and it's probably not possible for you to love them any more than you already do. But even in single-parent homes, if your kids are the center of your world, and the most important thing to you, you're doing a disservice to them.

It's only going to hurt your kids when they are the center of your world. I know it's a lot harder for single parents. You may have to split your time with your ex. That's tough. You want to give your kids everything when they're with you, which often leads to a lack of discipline, because you don't want any of the negative stuff when you have the time with your kids. Split living situations can also create two different sets of expectations for kids—if one parent is more minimalist and the other is more consumerist, for example. Or if one is trying to "buy" their children's affections, this may be an even greater challenge for the single parent.

Your kids may like the lack of discipline and the excessive presents when they're young, but they'll appreciate the discipline and healthy view of material possessions when they're older. I'm not saying to break out the belt when it comes to discipline (how you discipline is your choice and this is one topic I deliberately avoided in this book because there are so many other great books on the subject), I'm simply saying to hold your kids accountable. They can't get away with doing the wrong things just because you're a single parent and you feel bad for disciplining them. Too often, society lets things go because of the situation someone is in and that only hurts that person more.

Being a single parent is hard, but if it's where you're at, you have to face it. The good news is, single parents don't have to face it alone. When you seek Jesus and get involved in a good church/community, you'll get support. That support helps. Reach out when you need help, and find a good community of Christians.

## The Beauty of a God-Centered Home

When Jesus is giving his famous "Sermon on the Mount," he talks about not being anxious or worrisome. A child-centered home leads to both of those things. Center your home on God and watch how the other things fall in place.

It's not a magic bullet, and it doesn't mean life will be easy. Life is not easy. That's part of why we don't want a child-centered home, because kids grow up thinking life *is* easy.

A God-centered home gives you the strength to handle whatever is thrown your way. Let's look at a little more context in the verse just mentioned. When Jesus was teaching, he said…

> "Therefore I tell you, do not be anxious about your life, what you will eat or what you will drink, nor about your body, what you will put on. Is not life more than food, and the body more than clothing? Look at the birds of the air: they neither sow nor reap nor gather into barns, and

> yet your heavenly Father feeds them. Are you not of more value than they?
>
> And which of you by being anxious can add a single hour to his span of life? And why are you anxious about clothing? Consider the lilies of the field, how they grow: they neither toil nor spin, yet I tell you, even Solomon in all his glory was not arrayed like one of these. But if God so clothes the grass of the field, which today is alive and tomorrow is thrown into the oven, will he not much more clothe you, O you of little faith?
>
> Therefore do not be anxious, saying, 'What shall we eat?' or 'What shall we drink?' or 'What shall we wear?' For the Gentiles seek after all these things, and your heavenly Father knows that you need them all. But seek first the kingdom of God and his righteousness, and all these things will be added to you."
>
> MATTHEW 6:25-33

All of the build-up in Jesus' sermon leads to seeking the Kingdom of God so that, "all these things will be added." Jesus teaches, we should be content, and we should raise our children to be content. Gratitude and contentment are two of the keys to a fulfilled life, as we've already discussed.

It won't always be a happy life, but who ever said we should strive to merely lead a happy life? It's great to be happy, and happiness is part of life, but grief and sorrow are also part of life. Life is full of seasons. When we have a God-centered home, we have the strength to get through the gloomy seasons and the gratitude to appreciate the beautiful seasons. When we center our home on God, the love leads our marriage and our relationship with our kids.

God is the only one worthy enough to center our home on. The beauty is, when we do that, we become centered on what truly matters, and our life becomes full of joy... not mere happiness, which comes and goes, but lasting joy—through all seasons.

## Summary – God-Centered Home

It's not a child-centered world. If you raise your children as the center of your home, it sets them up for failure.

There are 6 reasons a child-centered home is dangerous:

1. It's not a child-centered world.
2. Your children will grow up thinking it's all about them.
3. Kids are automatically selfish.
4. You don't take care of yourself.
5. It's a burden on your marriage.
6. It puts your kids in charge.

Turn towards a God-centered home, not a child-centered home.

A God-centered home gives us the strength to get through any season of life, together, as a God-centered family.

SEVENTEEN
# INTENTIONAL DAYS
MAKE THE MOST OF YOUR FAMILY'S TIME

"The key is not to prioritize your schedule but to schedule your priorities."

STEVEN COVEY, AUTHOR OF *THE 7 HABITS OF HIGHLY EFFECTIVE PEOPLE*

"Take care of the minutes and the hours will take care of themselves."

LORD CHESTERFIELD, BRITISH STATESMAN

"Wherever you are, be all there."

JIM ELLIOT, CHRISTIAN MISSIONARY

If there is one question I get asked more than any other it's, "how do you find time to do it all?" And while I don't have the perfect routine, I'm proud of what I've created through working hard on my time management over the last 10 years. I've come a long way, and I have some insight into how you can fit everything into your day, without exploding from stress.

My life is busy, like yours. I'm active duty military, stationed at one of the busiest fighter-jet bases in the world, so to say I work a full-time job is an understatement. I also run two active blogs as a side business. Until I completed my Bachelor of Arts degree in Finance, I was also a full-time student. Additionally, I find the time to read, exercise, and spend many hours traveling with my family. Of course, there are times when I'm away for work (deployments, training, etc.), but when I'm home, I'm *fully* home, and when I'm at work, I'm *fully* at work.

So how do I fit all of this in without going mad?

One word: schedule. That's it. The end. Thanks for reading!

Ok, I'll explain. Here it goes, but before we go on, I want to make a quick point. I'm simply giving my perspective and ideas on being productive with a full-time job and a large family. I've studied the art of productivity. I've done my own experiments and research. That being said, I'm not perfect, nor is my life perfect. I'm going to share the things that have worked for our family, because I know they can work for yours.

## Calendar Vs. To-Do-List

*"Don't be fooled by the calendar. There are only as many days in the year as you make use of. One man gets only a week's value out of a year while another man gets a full year's value out of a week."*

CHARLES RICHARDS, AUTHOR OF *PSYCHOLOGY OF WEALTH*

This is the one thing, above all other things, that allows me to fit everything in. I have a to-do list, but that's not where the magic happens. The magic happens on my calendar. I know everything that needs to get done because of my to-do list, but most people stop there. Your to-do list must transfer to a schedule or you're never going to get it all done. A calendar is merely a to-do list with dates and times. You need to know exactly when you're going to do everything you're going to do.

As for my daily rituals, such as my morning routine, I plan it out to the minute—mostly because I think it's fun. If you're not a nerd, you probably won't think it's fun, but it's worth it. This is all about intentional time management. Of course, we can't manage time itself, we can only manage how we use the time.

Before I explain my mornings, we need to talk about this by-the-minute scheduling thing.

## Scheduling Every Minute

I schedule every minute of my day. You'll see what that looks like soon, but I need to make something exceedingly clear here…

*Scheduling every minute of your day shouldn't be stressful.* You shouldn't get anxious when something takes longer than planned, because something will. It's not a *hard* schedule. It's a *fluid* schedule. If something goes over the allotted time, change the rest of the schedule. It's meant to be a guide, not a law.

Whatever you do, don't let your schedule dictate your life.

Dictate your schedule. The entire point of creating a schedule is to gauge how long things will take so you know what you can comfortably fit in.

I started this by literally timing everything I did. I timed my shower, brushing my teeth, getting ready for work… everything. And I did it in a leisurely way to add a buffer. Now that I know exactly how long everything takes, I can plan around it.

It's funny how we misjudge time in our minds. We may have always thought we needed 30 minutes to get ready for the day, but when we time it, we only actually need 15, and that's if we're going slow. Or it could be the opposite. If you're often late, it's probably the opposite. Adding an extra 5 or 10 minutes could prevent you from ever being late again.

Scheduling every minute makes you intentional about what you spend your time on, and for the first few months, it really opens your eyes to how much time you spend on certain things. You never plan to spend four hours on YouTube or Facebook, but it happens. It shouldn't happen if you schedule your time. Now I'll show you some specifics…

Make the Most of Mornings

Use your mornings wisely. Mornings may or may not be the best time for you. I prefer mornings because I'm more creative in the mornings, and it's the only time my house is completely still and silent. If evenings meet those standards for you, use your evenings. I don't use the term "ritual" to sound enlightened or spiritual, I use it because "routine" is a boring word, and I don't want a boring routine. I want an intentional ritual.

Plan your mornings the night before. I've heard most people's brains are more creative in the morning, and more reasonable and analytical at night. Considering how much controversy there is over studies about mornings, evenings, and creativity, I'm not going to say this is science, but it seems to be true for me. Here's my standard morning (yours will vary):

**0300:** Wake up, make coffee
**0315:** Bible study and prayer
**0345:** Journal
**0400:** Write
**0600:** Check email (first time of the day—I only check it twice, at most)
**0630:** Get kids up and have our morning ritual (we'll discuss this ritual soon)
**0700:** Walk kids to bus stop
**0710:** Get ready for the gym
**0730:** Drive to the gym (listen to an audiobook on the way)
**0800:** Exercise
**0830:** Shower, get ready for work
**0900:** Work

I get more done before 8:00am than I used to do in a week. My evenings are relaxing, because of how much I accomplish in the morning.

What do your mornings look like?

Do they look like peaceful time together with your spouse and kids, or more like... chaos? Peaceful mornings are possible, but it takes preplanning. Let's talk about the ideal rituals you can implement with your family. Mornings should be something to look forward to, not something to dread.

**The Family Morning Ritual**

A productive morning ritual is well planned, which means you start planning the night before. If you preplan, you should be able to get up and go. Instead of spending your last few waking minutes on social media, consider using it to plan tomorrow morning.

As I mentioned, since most people's brains seem to be more analytical at night, and more creative in the morning, it's best to use that analytical brain to plan tomorrow morning, and then jump right into fun and creative mode when you wake up.

Get your children on board. Have them lay out their clothes the night before. Make the lunches and get breakfast ready the night before. You can do almost everything… the night before.

Before your kids reach school age, there's a good chance they're waking up on their own. They may not have a specific wake-up time, but they pop out of bed bursting with energy.

Once your kids hit school age, you'll likely have to wake them up. Some kids get up more easily than others, but it's important to train your kids to wake up well. When we noticed two of our children were sluggish and incoherent for the first 10 minutes after waking, we decided to change that. We spent a few weeks training them to get up and immediately get their brain working. Why? Because it's important to be alert as soon as you wake up, in the event of an emergency. If they won't wake up easily for school, they won't wake up easily for a fire alarm. Waking up well is a trained skill. Just ask any military drill sergeant—that's how I learned. I'm sure your kids would rather you, not a drill sergeant, teach them this skill.

When your kids hit the pre-teen/teen stage, it's time to put the responsibility of waking up on them. Get an alarm clock and teach them to use it. You'll still need to make sure they're getting up, but after a while, they'll get used to it.

**Morning Processes**

Your kids will need to brush their teeth and hair, get dressed, eat, complain about how early it is, and so on. You may want them to make their bed each day (a great habit to instill). They may even have chores to do before school. All of this needs to be organized the night before, especially if you have a house full of kids.

We create time slots that rotate our kids through the bathroom. If you have multiple bathrooms, this is easier, but it's doable with one. The girls can be brushing their hair in the bathroom, while the boys are getting dressed in the bedroom.

Our children always eat breakfast last. That's the best motivation to keep them on track. They never miss breakfast. But the funny thing is, before we started doing breakfast last, they would often be rushing to get their teeth brushed. Weird how that works. It reminds me of investing. Instead of "pay yourself first," it's, "brush your teeth first." You're getting the things they want to do the least out of the way first.

When it comes to getting dressed, pre-school-age children do best when their clothes are laid out for them. Kids ages 6-11 usually do best choosing from a few options. Kids 12 and older should be able to make their own clothing decisions (with your veto power, of course).

**An Idea That Works:** *Play peaceful music in the mornings (worship works well) for your kids to wake up to. Try this for a couple weeks, and you will notice a difference.*

**Family Breakfast Time**

Family dinners are fairly common, but a family breakfast? Yes, this is an essential part of a good family morning ritual. It's a great few minutes of family time to start the day. The key is giving yourself enough time to make it peaceful, not stressful.

Even if you don't all eat breakfast, this time of sitting down and talking before the day begins will boost everyone's mood. It also allows your kids to discuss what they have going on that day, and any coming worries or concerns. Feel free to add a "breakfast-table habit" of saying one thing you're grateful for each morning.

I don't have the science behind it, but mornings can be an emotional time for children—it's like they're more sensitive and their emotions are heightened. It helps boost their emotional strength by having some quality time before their busy day starts.

**Take the Stress Out of Mornings**

Mornings can be hectic and stressful, but you can change that. This is what works for our family:

1. **Wake Up Earlier** – You may be thinking, "but I'm already tired when I wake up." Waking up earlier won't make you more tired, and if it does, just go to sleep a little earlier. Waking up earlier gives you plenty of time to get everything done, including some of the things below. Since mornings set the tone for the day, make this a priority.
2. **Set a Schedule** – Since you're waking up earlier, you

have more time for a productive morning pre-ritual—before the kids get up. You'll be surprised at how much you can accomplish in the early morning hours, before the chaos wakes up.
3. **Reward Yourself** – Since you're scheduling some things during the silent hours, you should start your schedule with a reward. It's a reward for waking up early. This could be your favorite cup of coffee, some time spent on your hobby/business, or simply sitting alone to think and relax. If you have a lot going on, consider journaling, prayer, and meditation as they are all great parts of a morning ritual. [1]
4. **Stay Positive** – Once the kids are up, it's important to keep a positive attitude. Expect some things won't go as planned. Mornings often don't. Your positivity will be contagious and soon your entire family will start to become "morning people." Just don't be *overly* loud and cheerful in the morning… the Bible talks about people like that (Proverbs 27:14).

Don't let mornings be stressful. Take the stress away, and completely change your mornings so you can actually look forward to them. Once again, intentionality wins the day. Let an intentional morning ritual help you win your family's day.

## Intentional Time Management

I don't get on the computer after work. That's family time. We only turn on the TV if we're having a family movie night, but we prefer a family game night.

Occasionally, my morning ritual fluctuates. I don't stress to fit everything in, but there are times during the day I can use to save time later. For example, if it works out for me to do something productive on my lunch break, I use it wisely. However, I don't plan to have that time, because if I set it in stone and couldn't accomplish the task, I would stress out. It's more like bonus time.

We spend the weekends together as a family. We've downsized so much that we don't spend nearly as much time in the garage going through things we should've never bought in the first place.

If you rid your life of all the unimportant things that steal your time, and plan your days in advance, you can do all the things you didn't think you had time for. It requires effort to start planning this way, but aren't you trying to make the most out of this life? It's that intentional living we keep talking about.

A Weekly Family Schedule

Weekly planning is easy when it's just you—when you're the only person you have to worry about. With the blessing of a family, comes the difficulty of creating a schedule that works for everyone.

In the military, there are times—such as right now as I write this—when I am deployed for six or seven months at a time. Our family understands the importance of structure. There are things we do when we're all together that make it easier when we're apart… things like family dinner, nightly prayer, and activities throughout the week.

It's important for our family to keep that structure, especially for our children, in the midst of the unpredictable demands of military life. Weekly planning makes it possible to structure our life how we want it, and it takes out the stress of disorganization. Let's get into how we do it, and I hope you'll get some ideas for your own schedule...

The only way to get everyone on board and stick with a family schedule is by using a family calendar. And while digital is typically my preferred method for planning, a physical calendar works best when multiple people need to see it. I've used fancy calendars before, like the magnetic calendar that's on our fridge right now. However, you don't need to spend $100 on a calendar, unless you want the fancy markers and design.

I like monthly planners to give the entire family a good overview of what's going on for the entire month. If you prefer to plan a week out, you can find great weekly calendars as well. You could always get both: a monthly planner for an overview and a weekly planner for the specifics.

Finally, I like the idea of having a yearly calendar so everyone knows where to look for special events, vacation times, birthdays, etc. You can find affordable options for an annual calendar if you have the room for it (the garage maybe?).

Just by putting a calendar up, you're going to be more organized as a family. Start slowly by adding a few events, and eventually you'll get to the point where you have the family's weekly meal plan listed.

The more you can include on the calendar, the better. But again, don't get hung up on making sure everything happens in an exact timeframe. Be flexible with it. The entire point of having this calendar and schedule is to eliminate stress, not create it.

There will need to be adjustments. Go one week with a schedule, and then adjust for the next week. Once you get your schedule down, you'll be able to add and take away things that aren't serving your family well. And you can start including time for everything on the calendar.

Here are some things you may want on your calendar:

- Rituals (Morning/Evening)
- Study Time
- Homework
- Quiet Time
- Vacations
- Holidays
- Special Dates
- Chores
- Events
- Prayer
- Meals

Add or subtract as you see fit.

Do something today to plan your life. Buy a calendar, write things down, time activities. Starting is the hardest part. It won't be perfect at first. You don't have to get it right, just get it started. That's why you need to start today.

When we use our time intentionally, we'll often find that "more time" wasn't what we needed. We just needed more *planning*. As I write this, many people who are quarantined in their homes due to the coronavirus are finding out that more time wasn't what they needed. We can't wait until we're motivated to make changes and be intentional. Motivation follows action; it's not the other way around. Start implementing these things and the motivation will follow. That's how we can all live intentional lives.

Summary - Intentional Days

**How to Make the Most of Your Day**
You can make the most of your day by keeping your to-do list in the form of a schedule.

A routine is boring; a ritual is intentional. Daily rituals help to make your day flow naturally. Include your entire family in these rituals.

**Scheduling Every Minute**
Try scheduling every minute of your day. See if you like it after a few weeks or months.

The schedule isn't set in stone; it's fluid. Don't stress when your schedule gets thrown off. Mold your schedule to fit your day; don't force your way through each part of your schedule.

**A Family Schedule**
Take the stress out of mornings by following a schedule and planning the night before.

If you need more time, wake up before your children and get that coveted alone time.

Schedules will constantly need to be adjusted. Keep working at it. It's an ongoing process that may never end but being intentional in how you spend your time will lead to an all-around intentional life.

# AFTERWORD

My only goal in writing this book is that you feel led to live a more intentional life. Consider the "why" behind everything you do each day. I hope you enjoyed my story, my mission, and my book. I doubt you agreed with me on every point. I know I can be opinionated, but as long as I opened your mind to think, we both won. I promise to continue doing my own thinking as well, with an open mind.

Life is better when it's intentional. Intentional finances. Intentional parenting. Intentional living. I'm not sure if I can stress the word *intentional* enough, even as I've already said it five times in the first part of this paragraph alone. When we are intentional in our daily lives, we will get intentional results.

One of the greatest evils the enemy offers (whether you believe the enemy is the devil of the Bible, or what's commonly referred to as "The Resistance") is to get you so caught up in living your day-to-day life that you fail to live any of it with intention and purpose.

I strive to live with intention and purpose and I hope you will join me in that journey. Let's live an intentional life of growing, learning, and taking action.

Let's begin.

# RECOMMENDED READING LIST

I know the value of reading, but I also understand the value of your time. I've read over 400 books. Many were amazing and many wasted my time. We can only read so many books in our lives, so we want to make them count. This is a list I put together after much thought and consideration. It took time and these decisions weren't easy, but I can fully recommend every single book on this list. I've read them all at least once if not multiple times.

## Children's Finances

- *Smart Money Smart Kids: Raising the Next Generation to Win with Money.* Dave Ramsey and Rachel Cruze. Ramsey Press, 2014.
- *The MoneySmart Family System: Teaching Financial Independence to Children of Every Age.* Steve and Annette Economides. Thomas Nelson, 2012.
- *Make Your Kid A Money Genius (Even If You're Not): A Parents' Guide for Kids 3 to 23.* Beth Kobliner. Simon & Schuster, 2017.
- *Teach Your Child To Fish: Five Money Habits Every Child Should Master.* Holly Reid. The Master Playbook, 2016.
- *How to Raise Selfless Kids in a Self-Centered World.* Dave Stone. Thomas Nelson, 2013.
- *Raising Grateful Kids in an Entitled World: How One*

*Family Learned That Saying No Can Lead to Life's Biggest Yes*. Kristen Welch. Tyndale Momentum, 2016.

## General Finance

- *Dollars and Sense: How We Misthink Money and How to Spend Smarter*. Dan Ariely and Jeff Kreisler. Harper, 2018.
- *Debt Free for Life: The Finish Rich Plan for Financial Freedom*. David Bach. Crown Business, 2010.
- *The Automatic Millionaire: A Powerful One-Step Plan to Live and Finish Rich*. David Bach. Currency Publishing, 2016.
- *The Little Book of Common Sense Investing: The Only Way to Guarantee Your Fair Share of Stock Market Returns*. John Bogle. Wiley, 2017.
- *The Wealthy Barber: Everyone's Commonsense Guide to Becoming Financially Independent*. David Chilton. Crown Business, 1998.
- *The Richest Man in Babylon*. George Clason. Dauphin Publications, 2018.
- *The Bogleheads' Guide to Investing*. Taylor Larimore, Mel Lindauer and Michael LeBoeuf. Wiley, 2014.
- *The Millionaire Next Door: The Surprising Secrets of America's Wealthy*. Thomas J. Stanley and William D. Danko. Taylor Trade Publishing, 2010.
- *Your Money or Your Life: 9 Steps to Transforming Your Relationship with Money and Achieving Financial Independence (Fully Revised and Updated for 2018)*. Vicki Robin and Joe Dominguez. Penguin Books, 2008.

- *Kiyosaki, Robert.Rich Dad Poor Dad: What The Rich Teach Their Kids About Money - That The Poor And Middle Class Do Not!* Robert Kiyosaki. Plata Publishing, 2017.
- *The Total Money Makeover: A Proven Plan for Financial Fitness.* Dave Ramsey. Thomas Nelson, 2013.

Self-Help and Minimalism

- *Clutterfree With Kids: Change Your Thinking. Discover New Habits. Free Your Home.* Joshua Becker. Becoming Minimalist, 2014.
- *The Minimalist Home: A Room-by-Room Guide to a Decluttered, Refocused Life.* Joshua Becker. WaterBrook, 2018.
- *The 7 Habits of Highly Effective People: Powerful Lessons in Personal Change.* Stephen Covey. Simon & Schuster, 2013.
- *Tiny Habits: The Small Changes That Change Everything.* BJ Fogg. Houghton Mifflin Harcourt, 2019.
- *The Life-Changing Magic of Tidying Up: The Japanese Art of Decluttering and Organizing.* Marie Kondo. Ten Speed Press, 2014.
- *The Minimalist Way: Minimalism Strategies to Declutter Your Life and Make Room for Joy.* Erica Layne. Althea Press, 2019.
- *Minimalism: Live a Meaningful Life.* Joshua Fields Millburn and Ryan Nicodemus. Asymmetrical Press, 2011.
- *The Slight Edge: Turning Simple Disciplines into Massive*

*Success and Happiness.* Jeff Olson. Greenleaf Book Group Press, 2013.
- *Goodbye, Things: The New Japanese Minimalism.* Fumio Sasaki. W. W. Norton & Company, 2017.
- *The Magic of Thinking Big.* David Schwartz. Fireside, 1987.
- *10 Natural Laws of Successful Time and Life Management.* Hyrum Smith. Warner Books, 1994.
- *Eat That Frog!: 21 Great Ways to Stop Procrastinating and Get More Done in Less Time.* Brian Tracy. Berrett-Koehler Publishers, 2017.
- *Decluttering at the Speed of Life: Winning Your Never-Ending Battle with Stuff.* Dana White. Thomas Nelson, 2018.

## SPREAD THE WORD

If you found this book helpful, please leave a review on the site where you bought it. Or you could always leave a review on Amazon.com to give others more perspective on the book (it is the most popular bookstore, by far). Be honest with your review. If you found it helpful and want to leave a five-star review, great! Five-star reviews are my favorite. No surprise there. But I don't expect everyone to leave five stars, and I don't want you to feel obligated to do so, unless you truly believe it's a five-star book. I appreciate all the feedback I can get, so be honest with your review, and let me know the good, bad, and ugly.

Thank you for reading. It means the world to me.

# ABOUT KALEN BRUCE

Kalen Bruce is the founder of Freedom Sprout, a project to cultivate financial freedom for future generations. He has a mission to raise a generation of children who are financially literate and help others do the same. Kalen has been writing in the finance world since 2013. His work has been featured in *Simple Money Magazine* and in major publications, including *Yahoo! Finance, CNN Money, The Globe and Mail, The Penny Hoarder,* and *WiseBread*. He holds a BA in Finance. He has been married to his wife, Tiffany, since 2005. They have five children, and currently live in and travel throughout Europe regularly.

You can reach him via email at kalen@freedomsprout.com.

Check out the blog at FreedomSprout.com.

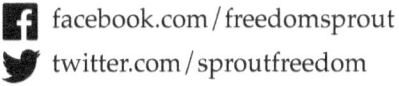

facebook.com/freedomsprout
twitter.com/sproutfreedom

# ALSO BY KALEN BRUCE

*10 Branches of Growth: Real-Life Productivity for a Fruitful Life*

I wrote this book as a guide for the 18-year-old me. It's everything I wish I would've known when I was just starting out in life. It's a manual for young adults.

## A Christian Productivity Book

I've read my fair share of books that tell me how to be successful, make more money, be more productive, and all the other things overachievers want to know. *10 Branches of Growth* is written with a Christian perspective in mind as we approach all of these topics.

Here are the 10 branches and how my book deals with each one:

1. **Character** – How character makes up who you are, what true character is all about, and how grit plays a huge role in your character.
2. **Discipline** – How to instill self-discipline in every area of your life by using 4 steps that are easier than you think.
3. **Action** – How to take action, do the work, and create motivation waves in your life.
4. **Habits** – The easy way to create positive habits, and how to change your identity based on your new habits.
5. **Energy** – How to increase your energy so you can grow the other branches, and how energy isn't just about sleep.
6. **Time** – How to control your time so it doesn't control you, and how to gain more margin in life.
7. **Wealth** – A real talk about wealth, and a simple method for budgeting and investing that works, without stealing hours out of your day.
8. **Seasons** – How to figure out which season of life you're in, and the importance of learning how to plan around your season.
9. **Self** – Figure out who you are, and increase your overall self-awareness to improve your whole life.
10. **God** – A transparent discussion about God, and the reason so many successful people are depressed.

You can get the book online at Amazon.com or any major book store.

# NOTES

## 1. Reframing Money

1. Kadlec, D. (2013). Why We Want—But Can't Have—Personal Finance in Schools. *Time*, October 10.
2. Harris Interactive Inc. (2012). The 2012 Consumer Financial Literacy Survey.
3. Huddleston, C. (2019). Survey: 69% of Americans Have Less Than $1,000 in Savings. *GOBankingRates.com*, March 16.
4. Katyal, S. (2015). Most doctors are financially illiterate. *KevinMD.com*, January 31.
5. Capital One and Consumer Action (2003). New Survey Shows Teenagers Want Financial Advice from Parents. *ConsumerAction.com*, October 23.

## 2. Teaching Money

1. For more on tithing versus generous giving, see my article, *How Generous Giving Replaced the Tithe (And Why Everyone Should Give)*, on FreedomSprout.com.
2. Pascarella, D. (2018). 4 Stats That Reveal How Badly America is Failing at Financial Literacy. *Forbes*, April 3.
3. Farber, M. (2016). Nearly Two-Thirds of Americans Can't Pass a Basic Test of Financial Literacy. *Fortune*, July 12.
4. *Debt.com* (2019). Personal Finance Statistics. August 26.
5. Kirkham, E. (2016). 1 in 3 Americans Has Saved $0 for Retirement. *Money*, March 14.
6. Amadeo, K. (2019). Consumer Debt Statistics, Causes, and Impact. *The Balance*, August 24.
7. Berchick, E. R., et al. (2018). Health Insurance Coverage in the United States: 2017. United States Census Bureau, September 12.
8. Insurance Information Institute (2019). Facts + Statistics: Industry Overview. *iii.org*.

## 3. Money Lessons

1. Anik, L., et al. (2009). Feeling Good About Giving: The Benefits (and Costs) of Self-Interested Charitable Behavior. Harvard Business School, September 10.
2. Philanthropy News Digest (2017). Charitable Giving to Grow 3.6 Percent in 2017, Study Predicts. Indiana University Lilly Family School of Philanthropy, January 13.
3. Valassis (2018). 2K18 Valassis Coupon Intelligence Report. Valassis Marketing Firm.
4. Pavlika, H. (2018). Viewpoint: Study Shows Coupons Change Buyer Behavior. Supermarket News, March 15.
5. For up to date statistics on debt, see the Federal Reserve's website at federalreserve.gov.
6. El Issa, E. (2017). 2017 American Household Credit Card Debt Survey. *NerdWallet.com*.
7. Ramsey Solutions (2018). State of Debt Among Americans. *DaveRamsey.com*, October 25.
8. Pritchard, J. (2018). How Manual Underwriting Works and Why You Need It. *The Balance*, July 24.
9. You can visit EveryDollar.com, Mint.com, and PersonalCapital.com to learn more.
10. Bach, D. (2016). The Automatic Millionaire. Currency Publishing.
11. Kontra, C. et al. (2015). Physical Experience Enhances Science Learning (study). University of Chicago, April 24.
12. George Washington University and Standard & Poor's (2014). Global Financial Literacy Survey.
13. Johnson, B. (2019). Active Funds vs. Passive Funds: Which Fund Types Had Increased Success Rates? *Morningstar.com*, September 20.

## 4. Work Ethic

1. Kobliner, B. (2017). Should I Give My Kids Allowance? *BethKobliner.com*, January 13.
2. Kobliner, B. (2017). Should I Bride My Kids for Good Grades or Behavior? *BethKobliner.com*, May 2.
3. Ramsey, D. (2013). Paying the Kids. Ask Dave. *DaveRamsey.com*, October 27.

## 5. Money Management

1. Debt.com (2019). Personal Finance Statistics. *Debt.com*.
2. Schroeder-Gardner, M. (2018). 10 Statistics About The Money Habits Of The Average American. *MakingSenseofCents.com*, April 30.
3. See DaveRamsey.com for more on the Baby Steps and his principles.
4. Board of Governors of the Federal Reserve System. (2018). Report on the Economic Well-Being of U.S. Households in 2017. Federal Reserve, May.

## 6. Transportation

1. Experian (2018). State of the Automotive Finance Market. *Experian.com*.
2. Cross, R. J. et al. (2019). Driving Into Debt: The Hidden Costs of Risky Auto Loans to Consumers and Our Communities. US PIRG Education Fund and Frontier Group, February.
3. Silver-Greenberg, J. and Corkery, M. (2017). The Car Was Repossessed, but the Debt Remains. *NYTimes.com*, June 18.
4. For the annual consumer report, head over to ConsumerReports.org.
5. Kelly Blue Book gives an estimated "Blue Book" value for vehicles. Head over to KBB.com to search.
6. CarFax.com provides the Car Fax report. Dealers will often pay for this. You may have to foot the bill for private sellers.

## 7. The Debt Trap

1. Van Oudheusden, P. et al. (2016). Financial Literacy Around the World: Insights from the Standard and Poor's Rating Services Global Financial Literacy Survey.
    *bbvaedufin.com*, December 2.
2. Debt.com (2019). Personal Finance Statistics. *Debt.com*.
3. Tsosie, C. and El Issa, E. (2018). 2018 American Household Credit Card Debt Study. *NerdWallet.com*, December 10.
4. Hayes, L. (2017). Living Paycheck to Paycheck is a Way of Life for Majority of U.S. Workers, According to New CareerBuilder Survey. *CareerBuilder.com*.
5. Prelec, D. and Simester, D. (2001). Always Leave Home Without It: A Further Investigation of the Credit-Card Effect on Willingness to Pay. *Marketing Letters*, Vol. 12, No. 1, pp. 5–12.

6. Chatterjee, P. and Rose, R. L. (2011). Do Payment Mechanisms Change the Way Consumers Perceive Products? *Journal of Consumer Research*, Vol. 38, No. 6, pp. 1129–1139.
7. Hershfield, H. (2012). The Way We Spend Impacts How We Spend. *Psychology Today*.
8. Peterson, B. (2018). Credit Card Spending Studies (2018 Report): Why You Spend More When You Pay With a Credit Card. *ValuePenguin.com*.
9. Atwater, P. (2014). Americans Are Getting Into Debt to Afford Food, Gas. *Market Watch*.

## 8. College Conversations

1. Julian, T. (2012) Work-Life Earnings by Field of Degree and Occupation for People With a Bachelor's Degree: 2011. American Community Survey Briefs, October.
2. Carnevale, A. P. et al. (2015). The Economic Value of College Majors. Center on Education and the Workforce, Georgetown University.
3. Pew Research Center (2014). The Rising Cost of Not Going to College. Pew Social Trends, February 11.
4. Streit, K. (2018). Mike Rowe Offering Scholarship for People Who Want to Go to Trade School. *DontWasteYourMoney.com*, April 12.
5. Hamilton, L. (2013). More Is More or More Is Less? Parental Financial Investments during College. *American Sociological Review*, January 3.
6. SEC Office of Investor Education and Advocacy (2018). Introduction to 529 Plans. U. S. Securities and Exchange Commission, May 29.
7. Flynn, K. (2018). The Truth about Scholarships and 529 Plans. *SavingforCollege.com*, August 27.
8. Dinkin, E. (2019). 40% of American Middle Class Face Poverty by the Time They Reach Age 65. *CNBC.com*, October 12.
9. SallieMae (2013). How America Saves for College 2013. *SallieMae.com*.
10. Calderon, V. J. and Sidhu, P. (2014). Business Leaders Say Knowledge Trumps College Pedigree. *news.gallup.com*, February 25.
11. U.S. Department of Education (1994). Undergraduates Who Work While Enrolled in Postsecondary Education: 1989-90. National Center for Education Statistics; Dundes, L. and Marx, J. (2006). Balancing Work and Academics in College: Why do Students Working 10 to 19 Hours per Week Excel? *Journal of College Student Retention: Research, Theory and Practice*, Vol. 8, pp. 107–120; Pike, G. et al. (2009). First-Year Students' Employment, Engagement, and Academic Achievement: Untangling the Rela-

tionship between Work and Grades. *NASPA Journal*. Vol. 45, No. 4, pp. 560–582.

## 9. Investing

1. T. Rowe Price (2016). 8th Annual Parents, Kids and Money Survey. *TRowePrice.com*, March.
2. Grow Your Capital (2016). Are Youths Ready for Financial Independence? Grow Your Capital.
3. After much research, it turns out that, in fact, all roads do not lead to Rome. Because oceans.
4. Weisman, M. (1999). The History of Retirement, From Early Man to AARP. *NYTimes.com*, March 21.
5. Lusardi, A. (2015). Financial Literacy: Do People Understand the ABCs of Finance? *Public Understanding of Science*, April 2.

## 10. Intentional Ownership

1. LA Times (2014). For Many People, Gathering Possessions is Just the Stuff of Life. *LATimes.com*, March 21.
2. Mooallem, J. (2009). The Self-Storage Self. *NYTimes.com*, September 2.

## 11. The Toy Trap

1. Jewell, S. (1999). The Nursery That Took All the Children's Toys Away. *Independent.co.uk*, November 11.
2. Dauch, C. et al. (2017). The Influence of the Number of Toys in the Environment on Toddlers' Play. *Infant Behavior and Development*, Vol. 50, February, pp. 78–87.

## 12. Ad Alert

1. Poulton, T. (2008). "Kidfulence" on Family Spending Strong: YTV Tween Report. *MediainCanada.com*, February 22.
2. Lagorio, C. (2007). Resources: Marketing to Kids. *CBS News*, May 14.
3. Campbell, K. and Davis-Packard, K. (2000). How Ads Get Kids to Say, I Want It! *The Christian Science Monitor*, September 18.

4. Homan, J. (2006). College Credit Card Statistics. *UCMS.com*.
5. Radunovic, L. (2014). Kids and Advertising: (Ab)using The Most Vulnerable Target Group. *Domain.me*, July 24.
6. Media Smarts (n.d.) How Marketers Target Kids. *MediaSmarts.ca*
7. Holt, D. J. et al. (2007). Children's Exposure to TV Advertising in 1977 and 2004: Information for the Obesity Debate: Federal Trade Commission Bureau of Economics Staff Report *ftc.gov*, June 1.
8. Wilcox, B. L. et al. (2004). Report of the APA Task Force on Advertising and Children. American Psychological Association, February 20.
9. Harris, J. L. et al. (2013). Fast Food Facts 2013: Measuring Progress in Nutrition and Marketing to Children and Teens. Yale Rudd Center for Food Policy & Obesity, November.
10. Horovitz, B. (2005). P&G "Buzz Marketing" Unit Hit With Complaint. *USA Today*, October 18.
11. Campbell, K. and Davis-Packard, K. (2000). How Ads Get Kids to Say, I Want It! *The Christian Science Monitor*, September 18.
12. Bernard, Z. (2017). YouTube is Reportedly Pointing Kids to Thousands of Disturbing, Violent, and Inappropriate Videos. *Business Insider*, November 8.
13. Maheshwari, S. (2017). On YouTube Kids, Startling Videos Slip Past Filters. *NYTimes.com*, November 4.
14. Media Smarts (2015). Online Marketing to Kids: Strategies and Techniques. *MediaSmarts.ca*.
15.

## 13. The Technology Threat

1. Influence Consulting Group (2016). Kids & Tech: The Evolution of Today's Digital Natives. *InfluenceCentral.com*.
2. Curtin, M. (2017). Bill Gates Says This Is the 'Safest' Age to Give a Child a Smartphone. *Inc.com*, May 10.
3. Khalaf, S. and Kesiraju, L. (2017). U.S. Consumers Time-Spent on Mobile Crosses 5 Hours a Day. Flurry Analytics Blog. *Flurry.com*, March 2.
4. Chen, B. (2016). What's the Right Age for a Child to Get a Smartphone? *NYTimes.com*, July 21.
5. Ungar, M. (2018). Teens and Dangerous Levels of Cell Phone Use. *Psychology Today*, January 16.
6. Suttie, J. (2015). How Smartphones Are Killing Conversation. *Greater Good Magazine*, December 7.

7. Fisher, J. et al. (2016). Technology Addiction: Concern, Controversy, and Finding Balance. *CommonSenseMedia.org*
8. Sabina, C. et al. (2008). The Nature and Dynamics of Internet Pornography Exposure for Youth. *CyberPsychology & Behavior*, Vol. 11, No. 6.
9. Ross, C. (2012). Overexposed and Under-Prepared: The Effects of Early Exposure to Sexual Content. *Psychology Today*, August 13; Owens, E. W. et al. (2012). The Impact of Internet Pornography on Adolescents: A Review of the Research. *Sexual Addiction & Compulsivity*, Vol. 19, pp. 99–122.
10. Stein, S. (2018). An Age-by-Age Guide to Kids and Smartphones. *Today's Parent*, March 21.
11. BioMed Central (2018). Social Media Use at Age 10 Could Reduce Well-being of Adolescent Girls. *ScienceDaily.com*, March 19.
12. Cohen, D. (2018). When Should You Get Your Kid a Phone? Child Mind Institute.
13. Lynch, J. (2016). U.S. Adults Consume an Entire Hour More of Media Per Day Than They Did Just Last Year. *Adweek.com*, June 27.

## 14. Growing Gratitude

1. Park, N. and Peterson, C. (2006). Character Strengths and Happiness among Young Children: Content Analysis of Parental Descriptions. *Journal of Happiness Studies*, Vol. 7, No. 3, pp 323–341.
2. Rothenberg, W. A. et al. (2017) Grateful Parents Raising Grateful Children: Niche Selection and the Socialization of Child Gratitude. *Applied Developmental Science*, Vol. 21, No. 2, pp. 106–120.
3. Halberstadt, A. G. et al. (2016). Parents' Understanding of Gratitude in Children: A Thematic Analysis. *Early Childhood Research Quarterly*, Vol. 36, pp. 439–451.
4. Algoe, S. B. et al. (2008). Beyond Reciprocity: Gratitude and Relationships in Everyday Life. *Emotion*, Vol. 8, No. 3, pp. 425–429.
5. Dean, J. (2016). The Dangerous Personality Traits on the Rise in the Young. PsyBlog. *Spring.org.uk*.

## 15. Rethinking Presents

1. Saad, L. (2018). Americans in the Mood to Spend This Holiday Season. *Gallup.com*, October 2.
2. Paul, K. (2017). Here's How Long it Will Take Americans to Pay Off Their Christmas Debt. *MarketWatch.com*, December 29.

3. Tuttle, B. (2009). Baby Hand-Me-Downs Are Suddenly Trendy. *Time.com*, July 9.
4. Hallowes, L. (2018). The New Birthday Party Trend that Makes SO Much Sense. *Babyology.com.au*, August 3.
5. Becker, J. (2018). Is It Times for Us to Rethink How We Give Gifts? *BecomingMinimalist.com*, November 23.
6. Grant, K. (2018). If You're Still Dealing with Holiday Debt, There's No Need to Be Scrooge. *CNBC.com*, November 20.
7. Martin, E. (2017). An Alarming Number of Shoppers are Still Paying Off Debt from Last Christmas. *CNBC Money*, November 17.
8. Magnify Money (2017). Americans With Holiday Debt Added an Average of $1,054, a 5% Increase From 2016. *MagnifyMoney.com*, December 28.
9. Finder (2018). Christmas Gift Confessions 2018. *Finder.com*.
10. *Ibid.*
11. The Week (2014). A Brief History of the Christmas Present. *The Week.com*, December 20.
12. Pham, J. (2018). 10 Celebrity Parents Who Don't Believe in Giving Their Kids Presents. *StyleCaster.com*.
13. SunTrust Banks, Inc. (2017). SunTrust Holiday Survey: Majority of Americans Would Give Up Gifts for Gatherings. *PR Newswire*, November 8.
14. Waldfogel, J. (2009). You Shouldn't Have. *Slate.com*, December 8.
15. Guillen, M. (2017). Why I Don't Give Christmas Gifts. *Fox News*, November 27.
16. A big thank you to Leo Babauta from *ZenHabits.net*. Many of these ideas came from the Zen Habits Holiday Gift Guide.

## 17. Intentional Days

1. *Lectio-Divina.org* is a great option for Christian meditation. It's the basic practice of reading a Scripture, and then praying and meditating on it.

www.ingramcontent.com/pod-product-compliance
Lightning Source LLC
Chambersburg PA
CBHW031100080526
44587CB00011B/755